Under God's Word

Under God's Word

Jim Packer

Lakeland

MARSHALL MORGAN & SCOTT

LAKELAND
Marshall Morgan & Scott
a Pentos company
1 Bath Street, London, EC1V 9LB

Originally published in the United States of America under the title
Beyond the Battle for the Bible by Cornerstone Books, a division of Good
News Publishers. Westchester, Illinois, 60153.

First published in Great Britain by Marshall Morgan & Scott, 1980.

The review of *Holy Scripture* by G. C. Berkouwer first appeared in the
December 1975 issue of *Eternity* magazine and is reprinted by permission of *Eternity* magazine. Copyright © 1975 Evangelical Ministries Inc.,
1976 Spruce, Philadelphia 19103. The review of *The Bible in the Balance*
by Harold Lindsell first appeared in *Crux*, December 1979, vol. xv, no.
4. Used by permission. The review of *The Authority and Interpretation of
the Bible: an Historic Approach* by Jack B. Rogers and Donald K. McKim
first appeared in *Crux*, March 1980, vol. xvi, no. 1. Used by permission.
Crux, is a journal of Regent College, Vancouver, B.C.

ISBN 0 551 00889 X

Printed in Great Britain by
Hunt Barnard Printing, Ltd., Aylesbury, Bucks.

To the memory of

Richard Coates
William Leathem
Alan Stibbs

three mighty men
mighty in the Scriptures

Contents

Preface

Debates about the Bible during the past century have centered successively 'on inspiration (so till Barth), revelation (so in Barth's heyday), and interpretation or hermeneutics (so since Bultmann took hold). Recently the so-called "battle for the Bible" has switched evangelical interest back to inspiration and the inerrancy which was traditionally held to be bound up with it, though hermeneutics is still the main concern of the rest of the church. In *"Fundamentalism" and the Word of God* (1958) and *God Has Spoken* (2nd ed. 1979) I have stated my own view of the nature and function of Scripture; I now offer this book as a contribution to the task of restoring the Bible to its rightful place in the lives of present-day Christians and churches— a task which extends beyond the battle for the Bible and which seems to me far harder to perform than that battle is to win.

Of these pieces, "Give Me Understanding" is based on two chapel addresses at Wheaton College in November 1979; "Inerrancy in Current Debate" was presented to a conference of the National Presbyterian and Reformed Fellowship in July 1979; and "The Use of Holy Scripture in Public and Private" is a

new version of material which the late Richard John
Coates collected in 1961, when he was Warden of
Latimer House, Oxford. Coates, an Irishman, im-
pressed his many friends as a cross between Winston
Churchill and Friar Tuck. He was an outstanding example of the well-read, deep-thinking, far-seeing
Anglican Reformed clergyman, shrewd, good-
humored, lucid, patient, common-sensical, happy—a
type less common today than once it was. It is a privilege to bring to light this specimen of his wisdom,
marked as it is by his love for the Anglican Prayer
Book and the authority of his own preaching, teaching, counseling and nurturing ministry, for which
many, including myself, still thank God. "The Bible
and the Church" has not appeared before.

As for the reviews, the first is from *Eternity* and the
second and third from *Crux*, the Regent College journal, with verbal changes.

J. I. PACKER

CHAPTER ONE

Give Me Understanding

You have heard of the battle for the Bible—who hasn't? You know what it is about—whether I can be a faithful, obedient, consistent Christian if I let go the total truthfulness—that is, the *inerrancy*—of Holy Scripture. You know, I am sure, some of the history that lies behind today's doubts as to whether we can trust the Bible or not. You know that for more than three hundred years God-shrinkers have been at work in the churches of the Reformation, scaling down our Maker to the measure of man's mind and dissolving the Bible view of him as the Lord who reigns and speaks. You know that in the rationalistic eighteenth century Kant, the fountainhead of most later philosophy, set the example of ignoring, as a matter of method, the possibility that Scripture is God's instruction to us, and leaders of Western thought have followed in his footsteps from that day to this, like a flock of sheep. You know that in the nineteenth century, dominated as it was by evolutionary ideas, the Bible was regularly downgraded, as reflecting times when religious thought was crude and unreliable in comparison with latter-day Western notions. You know how scholars labored to reconstruct the facts of Old Testament history from the "fancies" of Old Testament narrative, and to find the "real Jesus" amid New Testament distortions of him, and how men in the street boldly backed their judgment on all sorts of things against the witness of the written word. You know that in our disillusioned twentieth century folk are skeptical of liberal optimism and can no longer believe that everything is getting better and everyone is growing wiser and science tells us all we need to know. But you know too that neither biblical scholars nor philosophers nor the great mass of ordinary people have returned to the older confidence in Scripture as the revealed word of God, true and trustworthy because of its divine source and therefore able to give us the basic certainties about life and death that we need; and this despite all the efforts of Christians—call them conservatives, evangelicals, fundamentalists, as you will, the name does not matter—who have sought throughout this century to recall the church from worldly doubt to true faith at this point. These facts, which form the background of the battle, must by now be very familiar.

How should we regard this battle? It is a not-very-happy domestic debate among professed evangelicals as to whether we can keep in step with each other by proclaiming to the world and maintaining in our scholarship and ministerial training that Scripture is all true. My hope is that the fire which caused the smoke will prove to have been fueled by nothing more than attempts to avoid certain words, plus experiments in theological statement and biblical interpretation by a few scholars who, having tried out their ideas in print to elicit reactions from their peers in the usual scholarly way, will abandon them once they appear nonviable. But however that may be, a fight is on at present about these matters. Scholars are currently busy stating and defending their own views, and what in the way of constructive discussion may lie beyond this preliminary digging in is not yet apparent. Because evangelicals today have seen so many lapse from thoroughgoing biblical faith, and because they see how much depends on whether the Bible can be trusted or not, and because so many vested interests, denominational and institutional, are involved, feelings and fears often run high, and this could be dangerous in several ways. I focus now on just one of the dangers, that of so concentrating on the tactics of the battle as to forget the strategy of the campaign, and the kind of victory that is sought.

When a battle is on, those involved tend to think exclusively of winning, and to lose sight of the cause for which the battle is being fought. I recall the days when the Second World War was drawing to its end and Allied leaders began to say that, having won the war, our next and harder task was to win the peace. But not enough thought was given to winning the peace, and the record of the past thirty years proclaims that it was not won. In retrospect, it almost looks as if we forgot what we had been fighting for. I am afraid that something similar could easily happen in the battle for the Bible. So I shall now do what I can to ward off this danger, by asking you to raise your eyes above the battlefield and think about a series of strategic questions which pinpoint the significance of the debate for the theological and spiritual health of churches and Christians.

My questions were suggested to me by the Psalmist's prayer: "Give me understanding, that I may keep thy law and observe it with my whole heart" (Ps. 119:34). I should like to dwell on these words a moment before we go further.

Word and Spirit

How well do you know Psalm 119? Wise men come to know it very well, for they constantly seek to pray it. Why? Because it is a model, giant-size (176 verses long, twice the length of any other Psalm and ten to twenty times the length of most), of that on which wise men know that their well-being depends—namely, due attention to what God has said. The Psalmist celebrates the gift of divine instruction as "a lamp to my feet and a light to my path" (vs. 105), without which he would be wholly in the dark and unable to find his way. He hails God's word as the means whereby he comes to know, love, and serve the God who gave it, and he admits that he would in every sense be lost without it. His prayer for understanding springs from this admission, for he recognizes that to understand God's word—which means, to understand his own existence in the light of God's word—is to know the way of life, while lack of understanding is itself a state of death. Wise men identify. They see that the fear of the Lord which is the beginning of wisdom starts with the understanding that God alone can give. So they follow the Psalmist in cleaving to God's word and in asking its Author to interpret it to them in its bearing on their lives.

As writing, the Psalm dazzles. It divides into twenty-two sections, each marked by a different letter of the Hebrew alphabet, and each consisting of eight verses starting with that letter. All save one of its 176 verses refer in some way to what the Psalmist variously calls God's *word, words, precepts, statutes, law, promise, testimonies* and *ordinances,* which spell out God's *ways* and his *righteousness,* i.e., his revealed will for man, and the fertility of thought with which changes are rung on the theme of response to what God has said is amazing. It is a very clever composition; and it is more than that. It is a transcript of 176 distinct moments of devotion to God, and as such it is awesomely poignant. One wonders how far this heroic combination of ardor and humility, resolution and dependence, trouble and triumph, distress at the ways of men and delight in the ways of God, was realized in the Psalmist's own life (for Psalmists, like other poets, and preachers and prose writers too, could doubtless verbalize beyond their experience); one wonders if it has ever been fully realized save in the heart of our Lord Jesus Christ himself. Augustine's idea that the Psalms are essentially prayers of Jesus Christ is surely in place here, for what this Psalm shows us is the perfection of the perfect heart in its unwavering openness to all that God teaches in the Scriptures, and the Gospels show that our Master was mastered completely by what came to him from his Bible. So, in our measure, must we seek to be, for that is the way we are called to go. Jesus' disciples must be Scripture's pupils.

Psalm 119 is the Bible's own exposition, written in advance, of Paul's statement in 2 Timothy 3:16 f. that all Scripture, being inspired by God, is profitable "for teaching, for reproof, for correction, and for training in righteousness, that the man of God may be complete, equipped for every good work"; and Paul's statement is the Bible's own summary of what this Psalm is showing us.

"Give me understanding," prays the Psalmist. Under many kinds of pressure and in a turmoil of emotions he yet holds fast to the word of the Lord and rests his hopes in the Lord of the word. Distrusting himself and his own thoughts, however, he prays for understanding five times (vss. 34, 73, 125, 144, 169). He fears lest he should misconceive or misapply God's teaching, or narrow it unduly. He wants to comprehend its full range and thrust as it bears on his thoughts, purposes, attitudes, reactions, relationships, view of things and people; and he wants to comprehend it so that he may conform to it. "Give me understanding, *that I may keep thy law.*" Every day this should be your prayer, and mine too, for it is not enough for us to know the text of Scripture if then we fail to understand it, so that we think we are living by it when we are not.

The New Testament identifies the ministry of interpretation and application for which the Psalmist asks as the work of the Holy Spirit. The Spirit is "the anointing which . . . teaches you about everything" (1 Jn. 2:27), using as his means of instruction—his textbook, one might say—the contents of the Old and New Testaments. Understanding comes from the Spirit through the word; word and Spirit belong together. In Anglican prayer books, the collect for the second Sunday in Advent, based on Romans 15:4, reads:

> Blessed Lord, who hast caused all holy Scriptures to be written for our learning: Grant that we may in such wise hear them, read, mark, learn, and inwardly digest them, that by patience and comfort of thy holy Word, we may embrace and ever hold fast the blessed hope of everlasting life . . .

That for Pentecost reads:

> God, who as at this time didst teach the hearts of thy faithful people, by the sending to them the light of thy Holy Spirit: Grant us by the same Spirit to have a right judgment in all things, and evermore to rejoice in his holy comfort . . .

Each completes the thought begun by the other, and both are needed to express the full truth about the teaching work of God. More of that later.

I turn now to the series of questions which the Psalmist's prayer suggests that we who battle for the Bible need to be asking ourselves.

Authority

First, *why does inerrancy matter?* Why should it be thought important to fight for the total truth of the Bible? Some, of course, do not think it important, either because this is a belief they do not share, or because they do not regard others' disbelief of inerrancy as either dishonoring God or impoverishing the skeptics. I, however, am one of those who think this battle very important, and this is why. Biblical *inerrancy* and biblical *authority* are bound up together. Only truth can have final authority to determine belief and behavior, and Scripture cannot have such authority further than it is true. A factually and theologically untrustworthy Bible could still impress us as a presentation of religious experience and expertise, but clearly we cannot claim that it is all God's testimony and teaching, given to control our convictions and conduct, if we are not prepared to affirm its total truthfulness.

Here is a major issue for decision. There is really no disputing that Jesus Christ and his apostles, the founders of Christianity, held and taught that the Jewish Scriptures (our Old Testament) were God's witness to himself in the form of man's witness to him. There is no disputing that Jesus Christ, God's incarnate Son, viewed these Scriptures as such as his Father's word (see how he quotes a narrative comment as the Creator's utterance in Matthew 19:5, citing Genesis 2:24); or that he quoted Scripture to repel Satan (Mt. 4:3-11); or that he claimed to be fulfilling both the law and the prophets (Mt. 5:17); or that he ministered as a rabbi, that is, a Bible teacher, explaining the meaning of texts of which the divine truth and authority were not in doubt (Mt. 12:1-14, 22:23-40, etc.); or that he finally went to Jerusalem to be killed and, as he believed, to be raised to life again because this was the way Scripture said God's Messiah must go (Mt. 26:24, 52-56; Lk. 18:31-33, 22:37, cf. 24:25-27, 44-47). Nor is there really any disputing (despite poses struck by some scholars) that "God raised him from the dead" (Ac. 13:30), thereby vindicating all he had said and done as right—including the way he had understood, taught, and obeyed the Scriptures. So, too, it is clear that the apostles, like their Lord, saw the Scriptures as the God-given verbal embodiment of teaching from the Holy Spirit (2 Tim. 3:16 f.; Ac. 4:25, 28:25; Heb. 3:7, 10:15); and that they claimed, not merely that particular predictions were fulfilled in Christ (cf. Ac. 3:22-24), but that all the Jewish Scriptures were written for Christians (cf. Rom. 15:4, 16:26; 1 Cor. 10:11; 2 Cor. 3:6-16; 1 Pet. 1:10-12; 2 Pet. 3:16); and that they took over the Old Testament (Septuagint version) for liturgical and homiletical use in the churches alongside their own teaching. For it is also clear that, understanding inspiration as the relationship whereby God speaks and teaches in and through what men say in his name, they saw their own teaching and writing as inspired in just the same sense in which the Old Testament was inspired (cf. 1 Cor. 2:12 f., 14:37; 1 Jn. 4:6; etc.), so that the later conjoining of their official writing with the Old Testament to form the two-part Christian Bible was a natural and necessary step. None of this is open to serious doubt.

So the decision facing Christians today is simply: will we take our lead at this point from Jesus and the apostles or not? Will we let ourselves be guided by a Bible received as inspired and therefore wholly true (for God is not the author of untruths), or will we strike out, against our Lord and his most authoritative representatives, on a line of our own? If we do, we have already resolved in principle to be led not by the Bible as given, but by the Bible as we edit and reduce it, and we are likely to be found before long scaling down its mysteries (e.g., incarnation and atonement) and relativizing its absolutes (e.g., in sexual ethics) in the light of our own divergent ideas.

And in that case Psalm 119 will stand as an everlasting rebuke to us: for instead of doubting and discounting some things in his Bible the Psalmist prayed for understanding so that he might live by God's law ("law" here means not just commands, but all authoritative instruction that bears on living). This is the path of true reverence, true discipleship, and true enrichment. But once we entertain the needless and unproved, indeed unprovable, notion that Scripture cannot be fully trusted, that path is partly closed to us. Therefore it is important to maintain inerrancy, and counter denials of it; for only so can we keep open the path of consistent submission to biblical authority, and consistently concentrate on the true problem, that of gaining understanding, without being entangled in the false question, how much of what Scripture asserts as true should we disbelieve. Which brings us to our next subject.

Interpretation

My second question is: *Under what conditions can the Bible, viewed as inspired and inerrant divine instruction, actually exert authority over us?* My answer is this: Scripture can only rule us so far as it is understood, and it is only understood so far as it is properly interpreted. A misinterpreted Bible is a misunderstood Bible, which will lead us out of God's way rather than in it.

Interpretation must be right if biblical authority is to be real in our lives and in our churches. The point is obvious, but is not always stressed as it needs to be.

Have you ever noticed that we use the phrase "word of God" in two senses? Sometimes we use it to mean the text of Scripture as such, as when we call printed Bibles copies of the word of God. That is a natural usage, but not a strictly scriptural one. When the Bible uses "word of God" in revelatory contexts, it means God's message, either (as in the prophets) a particular occasional communication to some person or persons, or (as in the New Testament) the gospel, God's message to the world, or (as in Psalm 119) the total message of the Scriptures. My present point is that you can have the word of God in the first sense (by possessing a Bible, and knowing something of its text) without having it in the second sense, that is, without having understanding. The Psalmist asked God for understanding, and so should we, lest after vindicating Scripture as the written word of God we should still fail, as we say, to "get the message." Faultless formulas about biblical inspiration and authority do us no good while we misunderstand the Bible for whose supremacy we fight. The major differences between historic Protestants and Roman Catholics—papal authority, the presence and sacrifice of Christ in the mass, the form and credentials of the ordained ministry, the way of salvation by grace through faith—are rooted in differences of interpretation; so are the major cleavages between Christians of all persuasions and Jehovah's Witnesses, with their anti-Trinitarianism, their anticipations of Armageddon, and their legalistic doctrine of salvation; yet both Roman Catholics and Jehovah's Witnesses have historically maintained the inerrancy of Scripture (some Roman Catholics are slipping these days, but that is a detail), and have claimed that all their distinctives are Bible-based. You see, then, how important the issue of interpretation is.

Recently the more traditional guidance on biblical interpretation (well presented to us in such books as R. C. Sproul's *Knowing Scripture* and A. M. Stibbs's *Understanding God's Word*, published by American and British Inter-Varsity Press respectively) has been augmented by the academic discipline called *hermeneutics*. This covers more than principles for interpreting the text; it centers on the interpreting subject, and the way he comes to perceive and embrace what God is showing him in and through the text. It is an important field of enquiry, into which evangelicals do well to move. The rest of my questions in this discourse are in fact hermeneutical, and will show you something of the perspectives that hermeneutical study opens up.

Here, now, is my third question: *What are the obstacles to our understanding the Bible?* Obstacles, I suggest, can emerge at two points. The first has to do with the *rules we follow*.

A venerable but zany way to seek from Scripture understanding of God's will for you is the so-called *sortes biblicae* (biblical lots). What you do is prayerfully open your Bible at random to see what text catches your eye, or prayerfully pick out a text with a pin while your eyes are shut: both methods have been tried. Campbell Morgan used to tell of the man who followed this method and came up with "Judas went out and hanged himself." Finding these words unhelpful, he did it again and this time got "Go, and do thou likewise." In desperation he tried once more and this time the words that jumped at him were, "That thou doest, do quickly." Morgan's point (mine too) is that though this practice shows vast reverence for Scripture as God's means of communicating with us; it is of itself superstitious and wrongheaded, savoring more of magic or witchcraft than of true religion; it is precisely not understanding God's word.

Similar is the approach which detaches texts from their context to find personal meaning in them by feeding them into the world of one's private preoccupations and letting that world impose new senses on old phrases. Half a century ago a theological student, who later became a close and valued friend, had committed himself to start his ministry in a church in the North of England when he received a very attractive invitation to join instead a teaching institution in South Wales. He did not feel able to withdraw from his commitment, but one day he read in Isaiah 43:6 (KJV) the words, "I will say to the north, Give up," and concluded that this was God telling him that he would be providentially released from his promise and so set free to accept the second invitation. No such thing happened, however, so he went north after all, wondering what had gone wrong. Then he reread Isaiah 43:6, and noticed that it continued, ". . . and to the south, Keep not back"! At this point it dawned on him that he had been finding in the text meaning that was never really there, but had been reflected back on to it by the concerns which he brought to his reading of it. To impose meaning on the text is not, however, the way to learn God's law. Yet we constantly do this—don't we?—and it is one chronic obstacle to understanding.

There are basically three rules of interpretation:

First, interpret Scripture *historically,* in terms of what each writer meant his own first readers to gather from his words. This means seeing each book in its own historical and cultural setting, and putting ourselves in both the writer's and the readers' shoes. Each book was written as a message to the writer's contemporaries, and only as we see what it was meant to tell them shall we discern what it has to say to us. For the way into the mind of the Holy Spirit is through the meaning expressed by the men he inspired.

Second, interpret Scripture *organically,* as a complex unity proceeding from one mind, that of God the Spirit, the primary author *(auctor primarius)* of it all. The late C. S. Lewis was a virtuoso author who wrote criticism, literary history, philology, theology, apologetics, poems, novels, and fantasies for both adults and children, yet who expressed a consistent Christian viewpoint in all his varied output. If you were studying Lewis, you would look beyond the formal differences between one of his books and another to focus their common outlook. So with the sixty-six books of Holy Scripture, a library of literary diversity by more than forty writers put together over more than a thousand years: they too express one mind, telling one story about one God, one Savior, one covenant, and one church, and teaching one way of serving God, the way of faith, hope, and love, of repentance, obedience, praise, prayer, work, and joy. For academic reasons today's scholars draw contrasts, real and fancied, between one Bible writer and another, but practical Christians know that it is more fruitful in the long run to trace out how these writers blend. Scripture ought to be handled as an inspired organism of coherent truth, for that is what it is.

Third, interpret Scripture *practically,* which means (to use a precise technical term) *dialogically,* seeking always the word God addresses to you, here and now, to prompt your response to him. In Bible study we start as flies on the wall, watching God deal with men of the past, overhearing his words to them and theirs to him, noting the outcome of their faithful or faithless living. But then we realize that the God whom we were watching is watching us, and that we too are wholly in his hands, and that we are no less called and claimed by him than were the Bible characters. Thus we move into dialogical interpretation. Having seen what the text meant for its writer and first readers, we now see what it means for us. We study Scripture in the presence of the living God, as those who stand under both it and him. Each time it is as if he has handed us a letter from himself and stays with us while we read it to hear what our answer will be. To have this awareness, and to pray, "Give me understanding, that I may keep thy law," and then to read Scripture (or hear it preached, or read expositions of it) expecting Father, Son, and Spirit to meet, teach, question, challenge, humble, heal, forgive, strengthen, and restore you as you do so, is the crucial step in interpretation, to which historical and organic study are the preliminaries. John Wesley formulated it thus:

I am a creature of a day. . . . I want to know one thing, the way to heaven. . . . God himself has condescended to teach the way. . . . He has written it down in a book. O give me that book: At any price give me the book of God! I have it: here is knowledge enough for me. . . . I sit down alone: only God is here. In his presence I open, I read his book; for this end, to find the way to heaven. . . . Does anything appear dark and intricate? I lift up my heart to the Father of Lights. . . . I then search after and consider parallel passages. . . . I meditate thereon. . . . If any doubt still remain, I consult those who are experienced in the things of God: and then the writings whereby, being dead, they yet speak. And what I thus learn, that I teach.

Apart from the seeming narrowness of the phrase "way to heaven," which could divert concern from creative work for God on earth (though it did not so divert Wesley himself!), you could hardly spell it out more right-mindedly than that.

But now there is a second point at which obstacles to understanding arise, no matter how diligently we follow the rules. This has to do with *the blinkers we wear* (or *blinders,* as some North Americans say).

You know what blinkers are. They are the leather pads put over the eyes of street horses in the old days when carts and buses were horse drawn, so that the animals could only see a very little of what was in front of them. The blinkers narrowed their field of vision drastically, so keeping them from being startled by what they would otherwise have noticed happening around them. Similarly, blinkering factors may operate as we study Scripture; they may well keep us quiet, but only by keeping us from seeing what in fact we need to see. Let me show you what I mean.

You and I, like everyone else, are children of traditions, and hence are both their beneficiaries and their victims. They have opened our eyes to some things, and closed them to others. Most of us, I imagine, are children of Protestant, evangelical, pietist traditions in the different denominational traditions, Lutheran, Reformed, Presbyterian, Anglican, Brethren, Baptist, Methodist, Mennonite, Bible Church, or whatever. If we were reared Roman Catholic or Orthodox, the different traditions there will have left us different animals at some points from our Protestant brothers. The dispensational, pentecostal, covenantal, liberal, and other traditions of Bible teaching to which we have been exposed will also have made their mark, as will the inclusivist or separatist, large-group or small-group, institutionalized or free-style traditions of churchmanship to which we personally owe most. Being human, we shall see quite quickly how this shaping by environment applies to others at points where they differ from us, and be very slow to see that it applies just as much to us too. We have benefited from the traditions of our nurture and should be grateful. But we need to be aware that all traditions function as blinkers, focusing our vision on some things at which we have been taught to look constantly and which we therefore see clearly, but keeping us from seeing other things which other traditions grasp better.

Again: we are children, and therefore victims, of reaction—negative stances of recoil blinding us to value in the things we reject. Man's reaction never results in God's righteousness; it is not discerning enough. Thus, many Protestants have so reacted against Roman Catholic sacramentalism as to mistrust the sacraments entirely and in practice to deny their importance. (You could not guess from watching some churches that regular sharing in the Lord's Supper was prescribed by our Lord for his remembrance.) Reaction against the formalism and aestheticism into which "liturgical" churches can lapse has made some oppose all "set" prayers and all efforts after dignity in worship. Reaction against dry and heavy theology has made us woolly and wild, valuing feelings above truth, depreciating "head knowledge" by comparison with "heart knowledge" and refusing to allow that we cannot have the latter without the former. Reacting against yesterday's legalistic prohibitions regarding tobacco, alcohol, reading matter, public entertainment, dress, cosmetics, and such like, we have become licentious and self-indulgent, unable to see that the summons to separation and cross-bearing has anything to say to us in our society at all.

Sharing the reaction of our times against the past (we think of history as bunk, and of the latest word as necessarily the wisest), we cut ourselves off from our Christian heritage and end up rootless and unstable. These are just a few examples of how reaction, like tradition, can become a blinkering force, keeping us from seeing the value of sacraments, liturgy, theology, discipline, church history, and so on.

I am talking about what sociologists call *cultural prejudice*. I am saying that we all suffer from it, most of all those of us who think we don't, and that as a result we are constantly missing things that are there for us in the Bible. We are ourselves part of the problem of understanding because of the way that tradition and reaction have conditioned us. When, therefore, we ask God to give us understanding we should be asking him to keep us not only from mistakes about the meaning of texts but also from culturally determined blind spots. We cannot hope in this world to lose our blinkers entirely; we shall always be men and women of our time, nurtured by our own cultural milieu and also narrowed by it; that is the inescapable human condition. But we can at least be aware of the problem, and try to surmount it as far as possible.

Understanding

I can now pose my fourth question, which you might have expected to be my first, but I had to work up to it. *What is meant by "understanding"?* What is the nature of the understanding for which we should pray?

I have already hinted at my answer; now, to crystallize it, I offer you two pictures.

First, picture a *seminar*, as it might be conducted in universities known to me, and as I might try to conduct it myself in the college where I teach. There is a handful of students, all of whom are supposed to have done some reading on the day's topic, and one of whom has written an essay on it. The teacher has him read it to the class. Then there are two ways the teacher can go. He may choose to get the whole class dialoguing about the essay straight away. Or he may elect to dialogue himself with the essayist before that happens, filling in perspectives and, perhaps, giving some of his own reactions to what he has heard. Now imagine a seminar in which the instructor, himself an authority on the subject, is following the second course, and doing it so skillfully that you, a member of the class, can see at once from his comments on the paper what he would have to say about your present ideas on the subject. By his direct dealing with the essayist, therefore, he is actually teaching you a great deal; should the seminar end without you speaking a word to him or him to you, you will still go out wiser than you came in. This illustrates what I earlier pictured as our fly-on-the-wall relationship to God's dealings with Bible characters and his address in and through the biblical books to their original recipients. By observing and overhearing we learn what God thought of their attitudes, assumptions, ambitions, and activities, and what changes in their mind-set and life-style he wanted to see, and this shows us what he must think of us and what changes he must want to see in us. That is understanding.

Second, imagine yourself being *coached* at tennis. If the coach knows his stuff, you are likely to experience him as a perfect pest. You make strokes as you have done for years, the natural, comfortable way. He interrupts. "Hey, not like that; that's no good; do it this way instead." If you say: but I like doing it the way I did it, and it sometimes comes off, doesn't it? the reply is: doing it your way you can't improve; it's a bad habit, and you must break it. The coach will readily explain why you have to change; what he will not do is let you go on as you are going. He works for your good, forcing you to step up your game, and in your sober moments you are grateful. But he makes such a nuisance of himself that often you wish he would go and jump in the lake! This illustrates the fact that understanding is never abstract and theoretical; it is always understanding of the work and will of the living God who constantly demands to change us. What is understood is ultimately God's claim on our lives in virtue of all that he gives us in creation, providence, and saving grace. Notions about God's ways carrying no implications about our ways are not signs of understanding. Understanding, when given, is not always immediately welcome, for as W. H. Auden said in an appalling line—appalling not as poetry, but as stating something that is dreadfully true—"we would rather be ruined than changed." But God keeps at us!—and when, with the Psalmist, we set ourselves to keep his law by grace and make such changes as he requires, we know the benefit.

The understanding, then, of which the Psalmist speaks is a matter of receiving that *teaching* (first illustration) and that *reproof* and *correction* that leads to *training in righteousness* (second illustration) for which Paul said Scripture was *profitable* (2 Tim. 3:16). It means knowing as in God's presence what God's truth requires today in one's life. Such understanding does not come by mother wit, but is the gift of God.

Spirit and Understanding

This leads to my last question. *How does God give understanding?*

In Ephesians 3:16-19 Paul prays that "according to the riches of his glory [God the Father] may grant you to be strengthened with might by his Spirit in the inner man, and that Christ may dwell in your hearts through faith; that you, being rooted and grounded in love, may have power to comprehend with all the saints what is the breadth and length and height and depth, and to know the love of Christ which surpasses knowledge, that you may be filled with all the fulness of God." From this breathtaking prayer I draw the following answer to my question: God gives knowledge (= understanding, cf. Eph. 1:17 f.; Col. 1:9; understanding in this case of Christ's love, and how to respond to it) (1) through the Holy Spirit ("strengthened ... by his Spirit," vs. 16) and (2) through the Christian community ("with all the saints," vs. 18). Let me develop these points.

First, God gives understanding *through the Holy Spirit.* Yes, but that does not cancel the need for study, any more than it invalidates the rules of interpretation which we spelled out earlier. Never oppose the work of the Spirit giving understanding to your work as a student seeking it; the Spirit works through our diligence, not our laziness. As we saw earlier, understanding of what God's written word means for me comes through seeing what it meant when first put on paper, and applying that to ourselves. It is in application specifically that we need divine help. Bible commentaries, Bible classes, Bible lectures and courses, plus the church's regular expository ministry, can give us fair certainty as to what Scripture meant (and we should make full use of them to that end), but only through the Spirit's illumination shall we be able to see how the teaching applies to us in our own situation. So we should look not only to the commentators for the exegesis but also to the Spirit for the application, and to that end I commend to you three questions which you should constantly be asking as you read and weigh the sacred text. One: what does this passage tell me about *God*—his character, power, and purpose; his work, will, and ways in creation, providence, and grace? Two: what does this passage tell me about *man*—the human situation, man's possibilities, privileges, and problems, right and wrong ways of living, man in sin and man in grace? Three: what is all this showing me and saying to me about *myself* and my own life? Lift your heart to God and ask for the Spirit's help as you work through these three questions in the divine presence, and you will certainly be given understanding.

Fellowship and Understanding

Second, God gives understanding *through the Christian community;* not usually, and certainly not fully, outside the fellowship of faith. This aspect of the matter is not stressed in Psalm 119, but Paul's words, "with all the saints," point to it, as does his directive in Colossians 3:16: "Let the word of Christ dwell in you richly, as you teach and admonish one another in all wisdom, and as you sing psalms and hymns and spiritual songs with thankfulness in your hearts to God." Only as we gratefully share with others what we know and receive from them what they know will the word of Christ (the Christian message) dwell in us *richly* (abundantly and enrichingly), in the way that produces *wisdom.* Many of us are at a disadvantage here; we have had it so drummed into us that the only sure way to learn God's will from the Bible is to go off with it into a solitary place and dig into it on our own that we cannot easily accept that the interchanges of church fellowship, both institutional and informal, are the main channels of entry into spiritual understanding. But, though personal Bible reading is important for getting to know the text, and is the duty as well as the privilege of all literate persons, Scripture shows that the main means of learning from God is to hear his message preached and to involve oneself in the give-and-take of Christian fellowship in exploring the contents of Holy Scripture.

Don't misread me! I do not question the value of the many excellent schemes of personal Bible study that are available today; nor do I question the profit of continuous private Bible reading, day in day out, something of which I suspect most of us should be doing more than we are; nor do I forget that over and over again folk who had no biblical preaching within reach, nor any fellowship, have been wonderfully taught by God from Scripture alone. I am only saying that the New Testament expects that it is as we sit under the preaching and teaching of the word and share with each other about it, rather than as we isolate ourselves in spirit to commune with the Bible as solitary individuals, that we shall be given understanding most fully (and, with that, have our offbeat ideas and blinkered prejudices corrected most speedily). Again, I do not forget that a Christian may not finally surrender his judgment to anyone; the responsibility which Paul imposed when he wrote, "test everything; hold fast what is good" (1 Thess. 5:21) remains, and I must constantly tell you, with reference to all the views I express here or anywhere else, "I speak as to sensible men; judge for yourselves what I say" (1 Cor. 10:15). So now I ask you: do I read the New Testament right? Is it not in company with the saints in the church, around and under the word, that the apostles expect Christians to become men in understanding? Please judge!

If so, now, what follows? *First,* that you and I should take most seriously the preaching under which we sit in our churches. We should pray for our preachers as they prepare, and for ourselves as we go to hear them, and we should listen not to criticize but to learn, even when the preacher is not one of the best. *Second,* we should take most seriously the value of group Bible study as a means to personal understanding, and make a point of involving ourselves in it. *Third,* we should take most seriously the value of practicing fellowship with Christians outside our own circle by reading their books—including classic books from the Christian past, and expository books written from standpoints other than our own within the Bible-believing spectrum. (Thus, Calvinists should sometimes read books by charismatics, and charismatics should sometimes read books by Calvinists.) This will help us get some of our blinkers off, and see over the top of some of the ruts we are in.

Observing these maxims, and especially the third, will bring us a threefold benefit.

First, it will deliver us from the tyranny of *being tied to our own thoughts.* All our minds are narrower than we think, and blind spots and obsessions abound in them like bees in clover. Personal Bible study is always to some extent patchy and incomplete, for there is so much in each passage that we fail to see. We are unbalanced, too; those most interested in ideas focus on doctrine and forget ethics, those most interested in people focus on service and forget doctrine. We need the discipline of learning with the saints, past and present, in the ways noted above, to counterbalance our lopsidedness and to help us break out of the narrow circle of our own present thoughts into a larger vision and a riper wisdom.

Second, this procedure will deliver us from the tyranny of *being tied to our own time.* C. S. Lewis speaks of the "chronological snobbery" of those who care only to know the present because they think that only

3

34

the present is worth knowing. Such snobbery is found in both the church and the world, and in both it is a naive cultural conceit which needs to be punctured. The best way to puncture it is to get back to the really big men; reading the classics which in God's providence they left us will soon cut us down to size, and bring us a great deal of ageless wisdom into the bargain. So (for instance) if you want to understand the dimensions of sin and grace, you really must read Augustine. If you want to get the measure of the world of faith, you really must read Calvin. If you want insight into the life of sanctification, you really must read the Puritans—Owen, Sibbes, Brooks, Gurnall, Bunyan, Baxter and company. If you want to appreciate the height and might of God's work in revival, you really must read Jonathan Edwards. If you want to grasp what prayer is all about, you really must read folk like John of the Cross and that other giant of spirituality (for such he was), Martin Luther. The wisdom of these great souls finds us paddling in muddy shallows and takes us out to the deep things of God. It enlarges us spiritually as Sophocles, Shakespeare, and Dostoevsky enlarge us humanly. After every new book, urged C. S. Lewis, read two old ones. He meant two classics, and his advice was good. It is tyranny to be tied to one's own time and cut off from the wealth of the past—even if you are not conscious of it as tyranny. You and I will do well to break these bonds by keeping regular company with yesterday's great teachers.

Third, this procedure will deliver us from the tyranny of *being tied to our own heritage.* As we saw, we are all children of tradition (that is, of a particular heritage of teaching and training), and it is certain that the tradition that shaped us had a narrowing as well as an enriching effect on us. But we can start to neutralize that narrowing effect by learning to appreciate traditions other than our own. Some assume that their own tradition is all right and anything that is in any way different must be all wrong. If you are assuming that, think again!—or rather, start thinking now, for it does not look as if you have thought seriously about it at all as yet. What do you expect of traditions? Do you think of them as all corrupt, and of yourself as untainted by them, or do you allow that there may be good in them, as for instance in the tradition (denominational, inter-denominational, or whatever) which did most to shape your own present faith and life? The fact is that in each section of the church all the world over the tradition that has developed (teaching, worship patterns, hymns, style of nurture, etc.), whether viewed as definitive in the Roman Catholic and Orthodox manner or as merely provisional and pedagogic, which is the Protestant way, looks back to the Bible and offers itself as mediating the faith of the Bible. And since the Spirit has been active in the church since Pentecost, teaching and guiding according to Christ's promise, we should expect to find that at many points all Christian traditions mirror truth truly, even though at other points they appear flawed. Traditions are unlikely to be either wholly right or wholly wrong, but in the light of the Spirit's covenanted ministry we should expect them on the whole to be more right than wrong—and when we test them across the board by the Bible which they all seek to expound, this is what we find.

Imagine a millionaire or millionairess exploring a great department store, saying of every item on display which he or she likes, "I'll have that," and so piling up a vast stock of delightful purchases. That is a picture of each Christian's privilege in relation to the varied traditions of the different segments of Christ's one church. A well-known American reviewer (name withheld) has commended John Stott for not writing in a way that shows him to be an Anglican, as J. I. Packer does. Well, I am an Anglican, and there is an eclectic quality in Anglicanism which may have made it easier for me to see this present point, but the privilege of claiming as one's own anything in any Christian tradition that appears good and wise is a privilege that belongs to every Christian, not just to Anglicans. To enrich our own Christianity by ransacking the traditional wealth of all Christendom is open to each of us, if God gives us sense to do it. I for one know that I have been vastly enriched by authors and preachers, past and present, who were not Anglicans—more so, I think, than by those who were. I admit to thinking the Anglican heritage is as nourishing in itself as any in the Christian world, but what I owe to the Puritan tradition from Owen to Spurgeon and to the Welsh Nonconformist tradition in some of its latter-day representatives is more than I can measure. Both traditions seem to (doubtless blinkered) me to have had obvious blind spots of their own, but they have been vastly profitable to me nonetheless. I should like to think that other Christians were seeking and finding similar enlargement of understanding from traditions not their own.

Conclusion

To sum up: it is not enough to fight and win the battle for biblical inerrancy if we are then going to lose the battle for understanding the Bible and so for living under its authority. We must be clear therefore on the rules of interpretation, and with that be working constantly to get the blinkers off our spiritual eyes so that breadth of practical insight may be ours. If we want God to give us understanding, this is the way we must go. I ask you now to judge what I have said and if you agree with it to do something about it.

CHAPTER TWO

Inerrancy in Current Debate

The first and basic thing I want to say is: let no one
tell you (as some would certainly like to do) that the
inerrancy debate today is unimportant, a trivial
domestic squabble among those quarrelsome evangelicals of the U.S.A. On the contrary, you should see
the inerrancy debate as the latest chapter in a great
controversy about the Bible which has been going on
continuously in the church for the best part of the
last 500 years: a controversy centering in the last
analysis on the question, whether there ought to be
any such thing as evangelicalism at all. Let me explain.

The Evangelical Battle for the Bible

Evangelicalism, viewed substantially, may be defined
as that version of Christianity which affirms the
salvation of sinners by grace alone in Christ alone
through faith alone, as against any thought of salvation by effort and merit on the one hand or by the
working of ecclesiastical mechanisms, institutional
and sacramental, on the other. But evangelicalism,
viewed methodologically, must be defined as that
version of Christianity which determines its teaching,

attitudes, worship style, and practical priorities by expounding and applying Holy Scripture, which it receives as authoritative instruction from God the Creator, the God who speaks. The Reformed Christianity to which John Calvin gave definitive shape is, I judge, evangelicalism in its purest form, and it is the way of Reformed Christianity constantly to call for reformation of the church and its heritage, even its own Reformed heritage, by "God's Word written" (as Article Twenty of the Anglican Thirty-nine, my own church's confession, calls the Bible). Any principle, therefore, which has the effect, whether intended or not, of hindering Holy Scripture from exercising authority over the church in the manner described undermines evangelicalism, even if those who maintain it are themselves evangelicals at present in the substance of their faith and practice. For the principle in question can be expected sooner or later to erode aspects of their present belief, and to leave them with a confession which, if not positively false, at least affirms less than the Bible sets forth as being positively true. How serious this will be will vary from case to case, but that it will happen in some shape or form is, I think, inevitable. So the evangelical "battle for the Bible" which began, not in the nineteenth or twentieth century, but in the sixteenth with Luther and Zwingli, if not indeed in the fourteenth with Wycliffe, and which is with us still and likely to remain so till the Lord comes, has as its main concern the detecting and rejecting of all principles which would undermine evangelicalism by making it impossible for the Bible to rule the church.

A glance at the history will give us our bearings. What particular undermining principles have been detected and rejected in this battle during the past half-millennium? They boil down to four. The first

three, which form a group, were central in the six-
teenth- and seventeenth-century debates between
evangelical Protestantism, Lutheran and Reformed,
and Roman Catholicism. The fourth has been central
in intramural Protestant debate since the middle of
the last century.

Take the first three first. They are:

1. that canonical Scripture is not *identifiable*, but
needs an infallible teaching church to pick it out;

2. that canonical Scripture is not *clear*, even on
the most important things, but needs an infallible
teaching church to declare its meaning;

3. that canonical Scripture is not *sufficient* as a
guide for faith and practice, but needs an infallible.
teaching church to supplement it with "unwritten
verities" of oral tradition.

Now it is plain that, singly and as a group, these
positions make it impossible for the Bible to operate
consistently and systematically as judge and corrector
of the church's consensus and tradition, for at vital
points they make the Church's consensus and tradition decisive in determining what the Bible says, and
so in practice stifle its voice. (Think, for instance, of
what Scripture may not say within Roman Catholicism about the papacy and the mass!) No wonder,
then, that the Reformers rejected these notions.
What they affirmed instead can be crystallized into
four principles, as follows:

Principle one is about *communication* from God
through Holy Scripture. It is that the Bible, the written deposit of God's once-for-all work of revelation
and redemption in history, is the means and instrument whereby he teaches his people everywhere and
at all times all that they need to know in order to
serve him acceptably. The two million or so words,
Hebrew, Aramaic and Greek, which make up the Bi-

ble carry God's own instruction, embodied in the sentences and paragraphs of the books which he led his penmen to write. When the Reformers, echoing 2 Timothy 3:16, spoke of all Scripture as *inspired,* it was to this quality of being the God-given presentation of God's own message that they were referring. Calvin made the point by speaking (metaphorically and analogically, not literalistically and untheologically[1]) of God *dictating* the books, and of Scripture as coming *from his mouth;*[2] Luther made the same point before him by speaking of the Holy Spirit as the writer.[3] The basis of the Reformers' conviction that Holy Scripture is written communication from God to the world and the church was not tradition as such, though this view is certainly the traditional one, but the claims to, and acknowledgments of, inspiration which prophets, psalmists, wisdom writers, and apostolic authors voice in the text itself, plus the view taken and use made of our Old Testament both by Christ in his recorded teaching and in the New Testament as a whole.[4]

Principle two concerns the *extent* of Holy Scripture. It is that while there is no sufficient reason, historical or theological, for treating any existing books as inspired in the sense stated save the sixty-six books of our Old and New Testaments, both historically and in terms of the Spirit's confirming witness there are ample grounds for accepting these particular books as constituting the God-given *canon* (rule. norm, standard) for Christian faith and life. Apart from Luther's odd view of the nonapostolicity and therefore noncanonicity of James,[5] a view that rested on a misreading of James 2 and of which Luther seems to have convinced nobody but himself, the Reformers were together on the extent of the canon,[6] just as they were together in denying that one might lawfully supplement Scripture from ecclesiastical sources, at least in the realm of doctrine.

Principle three controls the *interpretation* of Scripture. It is that since all sixty-six books were written to be understood (yes, even Daniel, Zechariah, and Revelation) their main teaching must be plain and clear, whatever uncertainties of detail remain; and, further, since they came ultimately from one mind, the mind of God the Holy Spirit, they must be viewed as a single coherent organism of teaching given by narrative and exposition, example and illustration, an organism which will interpret itself from within through the light which each passage throws on others. Calvin was voicing this conviction when he laid it down that all biblical interpretation must accord with the analogy of faith[7] or, as it was later called, of Scripture—that is, the axiom that God-given Scripture is inwardly harmonious and must be understood and expounded accordingly.[8] When Anglican Article Twenty forbids the church to "so expound one place of Scripture, that it be repugnant to another," it is this principle that is being affirmed.

Principle four identifies the *authority* of Scripture with that of Jesus Christ. It is that Christ, the church's Head, rules his people by his word and Spirit—by the Scriptures, which all in one way or another witness to him, and by the Spirit who makes us see the implications and applications of the word which he inspired. Scripture is God's *sceptre*,[9] the instrument of his government; equally, it is Christ's *textbook*, from which as our prophet he teaches us how to honor and obey him as our priest and our king. Loyalty to Christ, our risen Savior and enthroned Lord, calls for total submission to Scripture, and anyone, or any church, declining to believe and do what is written there, or failing in practice to be faithful to it, is to that extent a rebel against Christ. In the *Institutes* Calvin spends much time showing that by this standard both Roman Catholics, who held to mediaeval traditions, and Anabaptists, who bypassed Scripture to trust supposedly direct revelations from God, were sadly rebellious in this way.

These four principles fix the status of Holy Scripture as the church's guide and judge, able to exert effective authority over the faith and life of God's people. In relation to Roman Catholic and Eastern Orthodox claims today, and to the reshaped Christianities which Protestant liberals and radicals, so-called, dredge up from the depths of their own religious sensibility, the same principles, I judge, still need to be enforced.

We turn now to the fourth obstructing principle which has had to be detected and rejected in the evangelical battle for the Bible. This is that canonical Scripture is not wholly *trustworthy*, since it is not wholly *true*. This principle arrived in Christendom relatively late: it first gained acceptance among mainstream Protestants towards the end of the last century, as a spinoff from Old Testament criticism and from a series of lives of Jesus which sought for the "real man" behind the myths and legends which supposedly filled the Gospels. Its essential assertion is that whatever inspiration we ascribe to Holy Scripture, it does not guarantee full truthfulness, either because inspiration means only the quality of having an inspiring effect on the reader; or because some parts of Scripture are not God-given witness at all; or because Scripture, being written by sinful men, is necessarily fallible, God having given his messengers only general thoughts, not specific words, and so confined himself to an inspiring activity that was partial, limited, and uneven; or because the biblical books prove on inspection to teach a series of incompatible theologies; or because the Bible says miracles happened, and we think we know they didn't; or for some other reason of that kind. The affirming of this principle by some, and the negating of it by others, has been the heart of the battle for the Bible within Protestantism for the past hundred years.

Though during that century Protestant leaders and institutions have succumbed to this skeptical view in large numbers, a succession of evangelical authors, of whom the late B. B. Warfield was undoubtedly the most distinguished, have constantly contended against its exponents, showing on the one hand that biblical teaching on inspiration entails the total truth and trustworthiness of all that Scripture says, and on the other hand that no compelling necessity springs from modern knowledge to conclude that Scripture errs anywhere: possibilities of its statements being all true and harmonious still remain open, and can often be shown to be likelier possibilities than that of their falsity. The work of Warfield's epigoni, the little men who follow the great man, continues today on both sides of the Atlantic, so that James Barr, the Scottish ex-evangelical, in his book *Fundamentalism,* can define fundamentalism as that brand of relatively conservative evangelicalism that holds to biblical inerrancy.[10]

The reasons which have led evangelicals to counter-assert inerrancy, despite the odium this brings on them from folk like Barr, are plain and compelling. Not only at the pastoral and evangelistic level does doubt about the truth of some Scripture breed doubt about the truth of all Scripture, and so make the church's task harder, but methodologically whenever one prefers a human idea to a biblical assertion one abandons the evangelical principle of con:tant and absolute submission to what is written, and indulges instead that habit of mind which has been the mother of intellectual arrogance and self-reliance in all its unlovely forms ever since the serpent entrapped Eve in Eden. Indeed, the point goes further, for he who makes his own judgment his ground for rejecting anything in the Bible thereby logically makes his own judgment, rather than trust in God's truthfulness, his ground for accepting everything in the Bible that he does accept. Stephen Davis, in *The Debate about the Bible* (Philadelphia: Westminster Press, 1977), makes himself look foolish by failing to see this. He claims to regard Scripture as infallible but not inerrant, and so writes: "I believe the Bible is or ought to be authoritative for every Christian in all that it says on any subject unless and until he encounters a passage which after careful study and for good reasons he cannot accept."[11] Comments John Gerstner, justly: "Davis's own infallibilist position self-destructs, for he admits that his Bible may even err on any crucial doctrine (though he hopes not and thinks it will not), and he admits that ultimate reliance for truth is on his own mind, Scripture notwithstanding (p. 70)."[12] That Scripture is not entirely worthy of trust is something which, as was said, has not so far been proved; but that any distrust of Scripture fosters pride, willfulness and confusion is something which both history and everyday pastoral experience have proved again and again.

It is true that during this past century, and especially since the rise of Barth and Bultmann, great stress has been laid on the *instrumentality* of Holy Scripture as the means whereby God encounters us and gives us knowledge of himself, and this aspect of things is the focus of attention in the discipline of hermeneutics as practiced by all fashionable Protestants in this post-Bultmann era. This modern hermeneutics builds on the axiom that though the conceptual content of Scripture, and the information and teaching we may properly glean from it, are matters of great uncertainty, yet God certainly makes an enlivening impact on us through the Bible, and the hermeneut's business is to understand this potent noncommunicative phenomenon of impact as thoroughly as he can. (A misconceived agenda? Yes, I think so, but we cannot go into that now.) Clearly, though, no stress, however strong, on the instrumentality of Scripture as a means of encounter with God can do duty for insistence on the *truth* of biblical statements. Where such encounter is affirmed on the basis that the biblical notions which under God trigger it off for us are no more than symbols reverberating in the psyche (and that is the common notion these days), the rot of subjectivism has already set in.

It was during the last-century debates on inspiration that the word *inerrancy* first became current in English, mainly at first among Roman Catholics, for whom it rendered the Latin *inerrantia*, and conservative Presbyterians in the USA. In Britain, then as now, the word was not widely used, but British evangelicals, led by such spokesmen as C. H. Spurgeon, J. C. Ryle, and H. C. G. Moule and relying on the work of such writers as Robert Haldane, Alexander Carson, and Louis Gaussen, stood firm for the reality of a wholly trustworthy Bible—and this, of course, is what matters, rather than whether or not they used this particular word. In this century, B. B. Warfield's exposition of inspiration as a divine superintendence guaranteeing freedom from error and mistake (an exposition no different in substance from that of Charles Hodge, Louis Gaussen, Jonathan Edwards,

François Turretin, or John Owen) has become virtually standard among English-speaking evangelicals
of all denominations both sides of the Atlantic, and
belief in inerrancy has gone along with it, as being
indeed part of it. Refusal to accuse Scripture of mis-
statement has thus become the hallmark of evangelical biblical scholarship, and the basis of academic
association in such bodies as the Evangelical
Theological Society in the USA and Canada and the
Tyndale Fellowship in Britain.

What this historical survey shows us is that all along
the line evangelicals battling for the Bible have been
after the same thing—the free, systematic functioning of Holy Scripture in the church as judge of con-
troversies and arbiter of what should be believed and
done. It was this concern which in the past prompted
rejection of all the four obstructing principles at
which we glanced, and it is this same concern that
prompts the rejection by evangelicals generally of the
idea that Scripture contains trivial mistakes. For two
or three decades now individual evangelicals have
flown this particular kite, and have generally been
howled down by their brethren for doing so. Because
the mistakes alleged were only trivial, emphatic hos-
tility to the suggestion that they existed has sometimes been ridiculed as a symptom of theological hys-
teria, a sign of neurotic and faithless fears, a case of
Corinthian contentiousness, and a lamentable example of making mountains out of molehills. But this
urbane view of the matter misses what the advocates
of inerrancy clearly see—namely, that as soon as you
convict Scripture of making the smallest mistakes you
start to abandon both the biblical understanding of
biblical inspiration and also the systematic functioning of the Bible as the organ of God's authority, his
rightful and effective rule over his people's faith and

life. We are now to look at some of the details of the inerrancy debate, but on the principle of not losing sight of the wood among the trees we should first fix it in our minds that the historic evangelical view of biblical authority, based as it is on belief in plenary biblical inspiration, is what the discussion is really about.

The Debate Reviewed

The current discussion of inerrancy began to take its present shape in the 1960s, when a professed evangelical, Dewey M. Beegle, published an attack on the notion (*The Inspiration of Scripture*, 1963; enlarged and reissued as *Scripture, Tradition and Infallibility*, 1973),[13] and the Second Vatican Council produced its Constitution on Revelation, affirming that "the books of Scripture must be acknowledged as teaching firmly, faithfully and without error the truth that God wanted put into the sacred writings for our salvation," but leaving open the question whether all that Scripture affirms comes under that heading.[14] About then, evangelicals were heard exploring the suggestion that Scripture might be inerrant only in what it *teaches*, not in what it *touches*—a line of thought parallel to that reflected by Vatican II.[15] Countering these developments came in 1974 what seems to me a very valuable set of essays under the title *God's Inerrant Word*,[16] and in 1976 Harold Lindsell's *Battle for the Bible,* to which *The Bible in the Balance* appeared in 1979 as a sequel.[17] Lindsell's books not only affirm inerrancy as a truth but chart the way in which in recent years particular churches and institutions in North America have lapsed from it and predict theological doom as the certain outcome of these lapses. Faculty members and associates of Fuller Seminary, one of Lindsell's featured institutions, produced an immediate rejoinder to Lindsell's first broadside, in the form of a special edition of the Seminary's house magazine, *Theology, Notes and News,* entitled "The Authority of Scripture at Fuller," and followed this with a set of essays edited by Jack Rogers under the title *Biblical Authority.*[18] Meantime the International Council on Biblical Inerrancy (I.C.B.I.) had been formed to sponsor exploration and exposition of the older view of Scripture in the light of the new situation, and in 1978 a symposium published under its auspices, entitled *The Foundation of Biblical Authority,*[19] worked again over the ground covered in *Biblical Authority,* coming up at several points with different perspectives and urging in particular that so far from being a problematical and possibly dispensable concept, as the earlier book had seemed to say, inerrancy was, in the words of the I.C.B.I. Statement of Purpose, "an essential element for the authority of Scripture and a necessity for the health of the church of God."

In the same year some three hundred scholars met under I.C.B.I. auspices to articulate the common understanding of inerrancy which they believed themselves to have. The resulting 3,000-word Chicago Statement on Biblical Inerrancy was signed by over ninety percent of them, and in view of this broad representative base of support it should be able to function as an agreed platform and reference point for the debates of the next generation.[20] It opens with a five-point "Short Statement" of just over two hundred words which is worth citing in full, for the heart of the matter is here.

1. God, who is himself Truth and speaks truth only, has inspired Holy Scripture in order thereby to reveal himself to lost mankind through Jesus Christ as

Creator and Lord, Redeemer and Judge. Holy Scripture is God's witness to himself.

2. Holy Scripture, being God's own Word, written by men prepared and superintended by his Spirit, is of infallible divine authority in all matters upon which it touches: it is to be believed, as God's instruction, in all that it affirms; obeyed, as God's command, in all that it requires; embraced, as God's pledge, in all that it promises.

3. The Holy Spirit, its divine Author, both authenticates it to us by his inward witness and opens our minds to understand its meaning.

4. Being wholly and verbally God-given, Scripture is without error or fault in all its teaching, no less in what it states about God's acts in creation, about the events of world history, and about its own literary origins under God, than in its witness to God's saving grace in individual lives.

5. The authority of Scripture is inescapably impaired if this total divine inerrancy is in any way limited or disregarded, or made relative to a view of truth contrary to the Bible's own; and such lapses bring serious loss to both the individual and the Church.

The next major item in I.C.B.I.'s literary program was the publication of the academic papers presented at the Chicago conference (*Inerrancy*, ed. Norman L. Geisler, Grand Rapids: Zondervan, 1980), and there is more to come.

North America has been the scene of the discussion as described so far, but we should note that some comparable happenings have occurred in Britain and Holland, not to mention Francis Schaeffer's constant insistence in recent years from his Swiss base that adherence or nonadherence to inerrancy has become what he calls "the watershed of the evangelical world." In Holland, recent appointments at the Free University, Amsterdam, have reflected a swaying conflict on the question, whether Scripture is all true, and G. C. Berkouwer's distaste for the concept of inerrancy, as expressed in his accomplished and impressive treatise *Holy Scripture*,[21] has caused consternation both at home and abroad. In Britain some reassertions of inerrancy have recently appeared, of which my own *God Has Spoken*[22] is one, and the Tyndale Fellowship, the biblical scholars' branch of the British U.C.C.F. (Inter-Varsity) network, has recently reacted to some publications of its own members by circulating a private memorandum which reasserts that belief in the total truth of inspired Scripture is one of the Fellowship's foundations and a condition of belonging to it, and requires periodic written subscription to the U.C.C.F. basis from all Fellowship members.

How much is at stake in this debate? Not much, say some; only the accuracy of biblical minutiae, and the limits of acceptable interpretation of some passages dealing with the beginning and the end of things, and the helpfulness or otherwise of a word linked in many minds with a rationalistic passion to prove Scripture true and an obscurantist indifference to cultural factors in interpretation. I think there is more to it than that, and offer the following analysis.

Questions at Issue

1. The basic question is semantic. *What does it mean to assert biblical inerrancy?* In some circles the word is espoused, in others shunned; for some it has a wide range of associations that are precise and good, for others its associations are uncertain and daunting. Words mean, of course, what they are used to mean, and no law requires us all to use them in exactly the same way, or to make any use at all of words which we happen to dislike. But as one who thinks that inerrancy ought to be asserted, I recognize that I have a

responsibility to explain what, in my view, the asser-tion when made should mean. So here are my proposals.[23]

First proposal: *to treat "inerrancy" and "infallibility" as equivalents.*

Etymology favors this: *infallibility* is the Latin *infallibilitas,* meaning the quality of neither deceiving nor being deceived; *inerrancy* is the Latin *inerrantia,* meaning the quality of being free from error of any kind, factual, moral or spiritual. Protestant usage favors this too: the words may carry slightly different nuances, *infallibility* suggesting that Scripture warrants a faith-commitment, *inerrancy* that Scripture under-girds orthodoxy, but it has been standard evangeli-cal practice for a century now to treat the words as mutual implicates. Attempts such as that of Stephen Davis to affirm biblical infallibility while denying bib-lical inerrancy[24] are the expedients of individuals with two convictional horses to ride—religious cer-tainty about the Bible's power, and intellectual uncer-tainty about its full truth. It would be a mistake to treat such deviations from ordinary usage as the norm.

Second proposal: *to see both words as safeguarding a particular procedure in interpretation.*

What are these words *for?* it is asked. What is their function? The immediate answer is: to declare that we accept as true what Scripture says. This is certain-ly part of the job they do. But the deeper answer to the question will surely be that we use them to declare our commitment to a way of interpreting the Bible which expresses faith in the truthfulness of the God who speaks to us in and through what it says and who requires us to heed every word that proceeds from his mouth. The procedure, best stated negatively, is that we should never (1) deny, disregard, or arbitrarily relativize anything that the Bible writers teach, nor (2) discount any of the practical implications for worship and service which their teaching carries, nor (3) cut the knot of any problem of Bible harmony, factual or theological, by allowing ourselves to assume that the writers were not necessarily consistent with themselves or with each other. The words safeguard this procedure primarily, and particular assertions which result from following it only secondarily.

Third proposal: *to see inerrancy and infallibility as entailed by inspiration.*

There should be no argument here. No Christian will question that God speaks truth and truth only (that is, that what he says is infallible and inerrant). But if all Scripture comes from God in such a sense that what it says, he says, then Scripture as such must be infallible and inerrant, because it is God's utterance. Any other view would involve watering down the meaning of inspiration unbiblically. So what our two words will express is not confidence that by our own independent enquiries we can prove all Scripture statements true (we can't, of course, and should never speak as if we thought we could), but certainty that all Scripture can and should be trusted because it has come to us (in Calvin's phrase) "by the ministry of men from God's very mouth."[25]

Fourth proposal: *to dissociate both words from unscholarly naivety in biblical interpretation.*

Critics persistently suppose that both words, highlighting as they do the divinity and consequent truth of the Bible, advertise if they do not actually signify a policy of minimizing the Bible's humanity, either by denying its human literary sources or by ignoring the marks of its human cultural milieu, or by treating it as if it were written in terms of the communicative conventions and techniques of the modern West rather than the ancient East, or by professing to find in it scientific as distinct from observational statements about the natural order, when scientific study of nature is less than five centuries old. It is understandable that Christians who know little of the differences between our culture and that (or those!) of the biblical period should naively feel that the natural and straightforward way to express their certainty that Scripture has contemporary relevance is to treat it as contemporary in its literary forms. Many, no doubt, have done this, believing that thus they did God service. But our two words have no link with this naivety; they express no advance commitment of any kind in the field of biblical interpretation, save that whatever Scripture, interpreted with linguistic correctness, in terms of each book's discernible literary character, against its own historical and cultural background, and in the light of its topical relation to other books, proves to be saying should be reverently received, as from God.

Fifth proposal: *to recognize that the words have confessional significance and a self-involving logic.*

By this I mean: let it be understood that for me to confess that Scripture is infallible and inerrant is to bind myself in advance to follow the method of harmonizing and integrating all that Scripture declares, without remainder, and taking it as from God to me, however little I may like it and whatever change of present beliefs, ways and commitments it may require. Both our words are often seen as belonging to worlds of doctrinaire scholasticism, but in fact they express a most radical existential commitment on the Christian's part.

Disconcertingly, G. C. Berkouwer, perhaps the most distinguished Reformed theologian of our time, dismisses the concept of inerrancy as a needless and misleading addition to the confession of Scripture as reliable and infallible. He sees this concept as bound up with mechanical ideas of inspiration, with unwillingness to take seriously Scripture's humanness and "time-relatedness," and with a misguided interest in making Scripture statements about the natural order square with modern scientific views. He thinks that talk of inerrancy keeps Christians from concentrating on Christ and salvation, which is Scripture's central theme, and that it trivializes the concept of error by putting scientific incorrectness on the same footing as moral and spiritual defect, and that on both accounts it hinders faithful hearing of the biblical message.[26] On this I comment:

First, if inerrancy implied what Berkouwer takes it to imply I should deprecate the notion too; but, as I have shown, I do not understand the word as he does. He quotes no sources on the perspective and motivation of the affirmers of inerrancy whom he has in mind,[27] which is a pity, for these pages of his otherwise fine book are so grotesquely superficial that one has to posit some personal trauma somewhere to account for their being written at all. Certainly, there is no reason to feel tied to conceiving inerrancy in terms of Berkouwer's morbid fancy.

Second, I agree with Berkouwer, as all Christians must, that the historical, space-time Christ is the goal and reference point *(scopus)* of all Scripture, but I see no incompatibility between acknowledging this and highlighting the truthfulness of Scripture in its presentation of the historical, space-time events by which this Christ came, and comes, to be known. Berkouwer's chapter 9, indeed, expounds the word *reliability* as doing just this latter job, thus making it in effect equivalent to *inerrancy* (in part, at least) as I and most others, I think, since Warfield have used the word.

Third, I think that Berkouwer himself misses the way in relating biblical to "scientific" accounts of created reality. In his proper zeal to get away from any thought that "Scripture teaches science," he seems to absolutize present-day scientific conceptions of the cosmos as "correct" and to adjudge the conceptions of Scripture incorrect by comparison, but in a way which, being natural, does not matter.[28] The right course, however, is surely to recognize that biblical references to nature and history, so far from being "scientific" in the modern technical sense, are simply declarations, naive, phenomenal, and nontechnical, about God in relation to the world of our direct experience; and further to recognize that they are expressed in such concepts of nature as contemporary culture provided (e.g., the three-decker universe, active consciousness diffused throughout the body, etc.), without in any way affirming or absolutizing those concepts, but simply using them as the apparatus and means for affirming something else—something about God's relation to his creatures, and theirs to him. This point belongs to the basic theory of semantics. By overlooking it, Berkouwer creates unreal problems.

Fourth, I find it a weakness in Berkouwer that in his admirable passion to spell out the theological and doxological meaning of Scripture he neglects apologetics, and leaves himself short of terminology for affirming to a skeptical world that the Bible is *true.* For this purpose the word *inerrancy* can be rather useful.

Fifth, I note with pleasure that Berkouwer declines to give up the word *infallibility* on the grounds that such a step would "contradict the confession of the God-breathed character of Scripture" and signalize on the part of the theologian "a transition from the reliability of Scripture to its 'unreliability.' "[29] That is exactly why I decline to give up the word *inerrancy*. My difference with Berkouwer, and his with me, is thus at this point neither motivational nor substantial, but merely verbal. I am glad the gap between us is no greater.[30]

I hold, then, to the understanding of what it means to assert inerrancy which I spelled out above; I deny that the assertion naturally or necessarily implies any of the theological crudities that Berkouwer rightly deplores; and I continue to believe that the assertion has its use, and that it is better at a time like ours to make it and then, if necessary, safeguard it rather than shrink from making it for fear of being misunderstood.

2. The second question concerns academic integrity. *Is not some obscurantism involved in affirming inerrancy in face of modern scholarship? Is not some measure of factual, moral and theological error in the Bible now proven? Should this not be frankly acknowledged?*

The idea that inerrancy has been disproved is on a par with the supposition that Darwinist evolution or Marxist social determinism have been proved true. All three notions are dogmas which many take for granted as certainties of our time; all three are spread by their own evangelists. But none of these fashionable shibboleths is proved beyond doubt, and men of integrity argue with force against them all. Concerning inerrancy, it is enough at this point to say: a responsible biblical scholarship exists today with inerrancy as one of its methodological assumptions. It is found among Roman Catholics (in dwindling numbers) and conservative Protestants (in increasing numbers). It produces commentaries, works of reference and other learned contributions, interacts with other schools of thought, and appears no less successful in making sense of the phenomena of Scripture than is its liberal opposite number. As long as Bible-believing scholarship can maintain itself in debate and show that skeptical hypotheses about Scripture are not the only ones possible, the real obscurantism will lie in saying that error in the Bible has been proved.

3. The third question relates to hermeneutics. *How does belief in inerrancy bear on biblical interpretation?* Interpretation rather than inspiration has been central for a generation in the world church debate about the Bible, and the modern touchstone for testing any proposed view of Scripture is to ask how far it helps to make God's message to us plain. What of the doctrine of inerrancy in this connection?

Here misconceptions abound. Many suspect, either for theological reasons or on the basis of their own observations, that belief in inerrancy makes against sensitiveness and insight in biblical exegesis, by loading interpreters with blinkering eccentricities. Disclaimers are therefore in order. So, first, it is necessary to disclaim the idea that belief in an inerrant Bible will render the believer an inerrant interpreter of that Bible. Nor, second, does belief in inerrancy imply that there can only ever be one legitimate option in elucidating a problem passage, so that he who takes a different view from mine, say, on the six days of creation may properly be accused, and in his turn accuse me, of not believing the Bible. Nor, third, will he who thinks his Bible infallible and inerrant take its human particularity less seriously than he who does not. The Chicago Statement speaks at length on this point, as follows:

We affirm that canonical Scripture should always be interpreted on the basis that it is infallible and inerrant.

However, in determining what the God-taught writer is asserting in each passage, we must pay the most careful attention to its claims and character as a human production. In inspiration, God utilized the culture and conventions of his penman's milieu, a milieu that God controls in his sovereign providence; it is misinterpretation to imagine otherwise.

So history must be treated as history, poetry as poetry, hyperbole and metaphor as hyperbole and metaphor, generalization and approximation as what they are, and so forth. Differences between literary conventions in Bible times and in ours must also be observed: since, for instance, non-chronological narrative and imprecise citation were conventional and acceptable and violated no expectations in those days, we must not regard these things as faults when we find them in Bible writers. When total precision of a particular kind was not expected or aimed at, it is no error not to have achieved it. Scripture is inerrant, not in the sense of being absolutely precise by modern standards, but in the sense of making good its claims and achieving that measure of focused truth at which its authors aimed.

The truthfulness of Scripture is not negated by the appearance in it of irregularities of grammar or spelling, phenomenal descriptions of nature, reports of false statements (e.g., the lies of Satan), or seeming discrepancies between one passage and another. It is not right to set the so-called "phenomena" of Scripture against the teaching of Scripture about itself. Apparent inconsistencies should not be ignored. Solution of them, where this can be convincingly achieved, will encourage our faith, and where for the present no convincing solution is at hand we shall significantly honour God by trusting his assurance that his Word is true, despite these appearances, and by maintaining our confidence that one day they will be seen to have been illusions.[31]

Fourth, it needs to be said that belief in inerrancy entails no commitment to treat all Scripture as con-

sisting of didactic propositions, and didactic propositions only, as if there is no more to it than there is to a
textbook of state law or an industrial rule book. In
literary terms, Scripture comprises narratives,
poems, prayers, parables, visions, and much else, be-
sides material with a directly didactic form. In logical
terms, Scripture's semantic units (sentences, paragraphs, units of discourse) are not only informative,
but illuminative, evocative, imperative, and sometimes performative too. Faithful interpretation,
among believers in inerrancy as among others, will
take account of all these things.

Should it now be said that making the inerrancy
claim seems to be more trouble than it is worth, in
view of the number of disclaimers with which one
must at once surround it, my reply will be that the
disclaiming of all these silly and perverse notions is
only necessary because liberals will persist in ascribing them to inerrantists. I do not think it will be
found that scholarly exponents of inerrancy have
ever espoused any of them, and if they have
appeared at the popular level it should be remembered that unscholarly exposition will mangle and
discredit any view whatsoever, not just belief in biblical inerrancy.

What positive help, then, can this negative-looking
concept give in biblical interpretation? Help comparable to that which Christological exposition was
given long ago by the four negative-looking adverbs
("without confusion, without change, without division, without separation"[32]) with which the Council
of Chalcedon surrounded its confession of one Christ
in two natures. In both cases the words operate as a
methodological barrier-fence and guide-rail: a barrier-fence that keeps us from straying out of bounds
and digging for the gold of understanding where no

gold is to be found, and a guide-rail marking out the way to go if we would understand what we believe more perfectly. Specifically, inerrancy keeps us within the bounds of the analogy of faith, directing us to eschew interpretative hypotheses that require us to correct one biblical passage by another, on the ground that one is actually wrong, and to explore instead hypotheses which posit a unity and coherence of witness at every point under the Bible's wide pluriformity of style. Only those who wish to deny that Scripture is the product of a single divine mind will doubt that this is a real and clarifying help.

4. The fourth question concerns spiritual health. *How does belief in inerrancy, or disbelief of it, affect the well-being of churches, clergy and Christians?* Space forbids the thorough discussion that this large question merits, and in any case the essence of what I want to say has been perfectly said already by J. Aiken Taylor; so I close this analytical review of the inerrancy debate by quoting without comment from his article in the *Presbyterian Journal* for April 12, 1978.

> The lively issue of Bible inerrancy today is very little a matter of whether one can or cannot find contradictions in the Bible. It is very much a matter of how respectfully one is prepared to treat the material found in the pages of Holy Writ. . . .
>
> The essence of the argument is not whether one can or cannot prove or disprove contradictions and errors in Scripture. Millions of words are being wasted on efforts to eliminate alleged contradictions through textual criticism, archaeological findings, interpretative principles. Such efforts are fruitless because one finally is dealing with a foundational attitude toward Scripture and not with the text of Scripture.
>
> The issue is one of faith, not scholarship. . . .
>
> The debate on inerrancy must go on, for it is foundational to any other debate. . . .

At issue is personal spiritual maturity, power in wit-nessing, and the entire integrity of the Church.

Many a minister, discouraged in his own spiritual experience and by the fruitlessness of his ministry, would find the answer in the measure of his commitment to the Word of God—if he looked. The necessary step is one of faith, just as the first step of commitment to Christ is one of faith.

One does not pray, "God, help me resolve the seeming contradictions I have found in the Bible." One rather prays, "God, help me to receive Thy Word wholly, unquestioningly, obediently. Let me make it indeed and altogether *the* lamp unto my feet and the light unto my pathway."[33]

Without comment, did I say? Let me at least allow myself to cry, Amen!

CHAPTER THREE

The Use of Holy Scripture in Public and Private

R. J. Coates and J. I. Packer

A well-worn Bible is an impressive if not a beautiful sight. Its much-thumbed parts reveal its owner's favorite pastures, and are eloquent of the blessings and battles of his Christian life. Such Bibles are not so common today as in former generations. In many homes, the Bible, like Shakespeare, rests quietly in the family bookcase, both volumes bearing mute testimony, by their cleanness and stiff bindings, to an entire neglect of their contents. The Bible still sells well, particularly in new translations, but on the whole it seems to be less and less read.

The disuse of the Bible in homes may be attributed simply to the general decline in religious observance in our day. But if we are to seek for causes as well as study symptoms we must go deeper and relate this fate to certain significant features which have marked church life during the last eighty years. The use of the Bible has largely ceased in the pulpit and pew, as well as in the home. The preacher with Bible in hand, referring to Scripture as he goes along, is nowadays an unusual sight, and as a direct conse-quence the listener has no Bible in his hand either. He has learned that he is not likely to need one, since preachers make so little obvious reference to Scripture. The lectern Bible is still the only copy of the word of God to be seen in many churches, even during public worship. The Sunday School, where it still exists, may boast many visual aids, and of course the stories taught will generally come from the Bible, but the Bible itself in the teacher's hand as authority and inspiration is nowadays often missing. Within the church, as well as among those without who do not attend, though the Bible is revered in a vague and general way, its riches are unknown, and its contents are no longer common coin and daily bread among the people of God.

We can be thankful that there is today a movement of return to the Bible. For too long the Bible has been in the dock, on trial, without its own voice ever being heard. In the common mind it has been discredited by the advances of science. In the church it has been too often dismembered by its critical students. Thus its testimony has been silenced by some and mutilated by others. We need again to recognize that the place for the Bible is not in the dock, nor even in the witness stand, but on the judgment seat, on the Throne, as the word of the Eternal. God has "magnified" his "word" above all his "name" (Ps. 138:21, KJV), for it is the revelation of his name; without it we abide in darkness and ignorance, and do not know him.

In what follows, we approach the subject of the use and study of the Bible from the standpoint of a simple acceptance of it as Holy Scripture, the written word of God. The modern neglect of it, of which we have spoken, has led to great failures in understanding it. Many feel competent nowadays to adjudicate on its worth who have never attempted to master its contents, or to live by its message. The caricatures

which otherwise well-informed people accept as true
pictures of Christian belief could only gain currency
in a society which errs because it knows "neither the
scriptures, nor the power of God" (Mt. 22:29). In
many ways the task that confronts us in seeking to
restore the proper use of the Bible is similar to that
which challenged the leaders of reform in the sixteenth century. We have, however, many advantages
over them, not the least being our inheritance of
their principles, embodied as they have been in the life
and worship of Protestant churches over the centuries. We do not have to create a tradition, or to
appeal, as the Reformers had to do, to the tradition
of the primitive church, a tradition beyond the ken of
all but a few scholars. Our task is rather to revive a
tradition which has never, even in our day, been
without some living exponents of its worth. It is the
results of careless neglect rather than total unaware-
ness of what should be that we have to combat.

The Bible in the Church

It was the intention of Archbishop Cranmer and his
fellow Reformers that the Bible and the Prayer Book,
two volumes available to all, should provide the
Church of England with everything that it needed for
its life and worship and growth. The Prayer Book
replaced the many corrupt and confusing service
books which had been used in mediaeval times. It was
a book which sought to return so far as was convenient and edifying to primitive practice, though it
incorporated new material together with what was
traditional. It was compiled for the English nation
alone, and it was made clear that it could be altered
when desirable to suit changed times and circumstances. Its aim was to provide the English Church
with forms of worship which should be at once bibli-

cal, edifying, appropriate, and, so far as was consistent with these primary requirements, primitive and traditional. Cranmer's cardinal principle in constructing it, a principle which should be recognized in every liturgy, was that the pure word of God, the text of Holy Scripture, must be constantly read, and only such forms and ceremonies might be used as were agreeable to its teaching. Bible reading and instruction formed the backbone of the liturgy, and the forms of response in praise, prayer, and thanksgiving were fashioned in the thoughts and terms of Scripture. Take the Bible passages out of the English liturgy, and it collapses. Take from the remainder everything that can be traced to scriptural sources, and you have virtually nothing left. For the Prayer Book was built out of the Bible itself.

Were the Reformers justified in their slavish adherence to the conception of Bible reading as the fundamental requirement of spiritual worship? After all, there is very little in the New Testament about Bible reading. Obviously, there could not be exhortations to read as Holy Scripture books which were still being written, or still to be written. But the fact that the New Testament Scriptures came later in time than the first founding of the church might suggest the superficial judgment that, since the church managed to exist before the Gospels and Epistles were written, its life could never be dependent on them. A little reflection, however, shows that this conclusion is fallacious. While the New Testament says nothing about reading any of the books of the New Testament (save in 2 Peter 3:15 f., where Paul's letters are implicitly commended for study as Scripture), it contains teaching which is very significant in this connection about the preaching and hearing of the word of God. This phrase, "the word of God," in the New

Testament regularly denotes the gospel. The church came into being through proclamation of the gospel. It grew through persistent preaching of the gospel to the unconverted. Its life was sustained by men divinely gifted to expound and apply gospel truth. All the functions of the ministry in the New Testament (see 1 Cor. 12:28, Eph. 4:11) have to do with preaching or teaching the divine word (the primary form of ministry), or with pastoral care according to the requirements of that word. There is a significant absence of any reference to priestly or sacerdotal duties. The apostolic ministry, as the very name implies, was and is a messenger's ministry, a ministry of men sent with a message from God. The church was born, and lived, through the preaching of the apostles. And it is precisely the substance of this life-giving preaching which we have in written form in the New Testament.

It is true that the apostolic message prescribed as a matter of integral importance the administration of the rites of Baptism and the Lord's Supper. But these sacramental observances are subsidiary instruments of the word. It is only in the context of its proclamation and reception that they can be rightly used. It is notable that, in terms of quantity, the New Testament writings contain comparatively little teaching on the two sacraments of the gospel, and very little indeed on the Lord's Supper. (This is not, of course, to deny that they contain much on the spiritual truths which the sacraments show forth.) Various explanations have been offered for this apparent neglect of sacramental teaching by those who find the New Testament proportions an embarrassment, but the obvious explanation would appear to be that the truths which the sacraments teach and the blessings which they convey are clearly and effectively exhibited and received through the word of God itself, preached and trusted. The great and fundamental means of grace is God's message, his word. The sacraments, rightly received, function as means of grace in their character as visible words, significant signs of gospel promises. But no New Testament writer would look upon the sacraments as exclusive means of receiving spiritual blessings which were not otherwise attainable. The sacraments have a vital place in the church, but it is a place subordinate to the word. The sacraments serve the word; they minister blessing precisely by ministering the word. To the earliest converts, they were visible tokens, pledges, and certifications of the gospel blessings which the less tangible, but more abiding, word of the Lord had brought within the grasp of their faith.

Another significant feature of the life of the church in apostolic times is worthy of comment. When, with the increasing number of converts to the faith, problems of practical pastoral care arose, Peter and the other apostles asked the church to choose others to do their lesser work, since they had to give themselves wholly to the primary tasks of preaching the word of God and of prayer (Acts 6:4). Social concern, necessary as it was, and natural as it is where the gospel is preached, as the early chapters of Acts testify, was not allowed to interfere with the primary function by which the church lives. Social application of the principles of the gospel must not usurp the primacy of the task of publishing the message of salvation from sin. The apostolic priorities, the word and prayer, have often since those early days been neglected in the interests of the widows and the orphans. Of course, there need not be any conflict between these two concerns; but both will be better fulfilled when the correct order is maintained. Recent history, however, has shown us that the "social gospel" can sometimes steal the place of the gospel of the grace of Christ, and the study of economic programs may flourish over the covers of a neglected Bible.

The suggestion that the Bible cannot merit the pre-eminent place in the church's life which the Reformers gave it, because the written New Testament followed and did not precede the founding of the church, is fallacious in a second way. The picture of the Reformed pastor, with Bible in hand, as the true and faithful successor of the apostles calls attention to a truth of great importance. Our Lord and the apostles and the early church had a Bible—the Old Testament. Though the first Christian preachers did not carry it around in their hands, it was always on their lips, and written too in their hearts and consciences, as foretelling, explaining, and confirming the good news of Jesus the Messiah. No teacher could hope to receive much credence in a Jewish community at that time who did not follow the method of starting from the Old Testament Scriptures. The Jews accepted the Law, the Prophets, and the Writings as "God's Word written" (the phrase is from Article Twenty), and would not knowingly countenance teaching that was not in some way based on these documents. But the gospel was sent "to the Jew first"; and it was preached to the Jews, as it was learned by the Gentiles, from the Scriptures. The opening of our Lord's ministry in his home synagogue at Nazareth presents a typical scene which must have been repeated often in the early days of the church—namely, the reciting of prophetic Scriptures, followed by the declaration of their fulfillment, as on that occasion our Lord announced that Isaiah 61:1 ff. was being fulfilled in him and his ministry. (See Luke 4:16 ff.; cf. Acts 13:14 ff.)

Here we see the technique (if we may use the word)

of a great deal of our Lord's ministry: to read or recall the Sripture, to explain, amplify, and apply it, to correct misinterpretations commonly held, or backed by ecclesiastical tradition, and to challenge men to face its true meaning. He used this method again after his resurrection to speak to the hearts of his despondent disciples on the Emmaus road—"beginning at Moses and all the Prophets, he interpreted to them in all the scriptures the things concerning himself" (Luke 24:27). Later that day, he appeared to all the disciples in the upper room in Jerusalem, and in similar manner enlightened them, and commanded them to proclaim the message of repentance and remission of sins. The passage is so important that we must quote it at length.

> Then he said to them, "These are my words which I spoke to you, while I was still with you, that everything written about me in the law of Moses and the prophets and the psalms must be fulfilled." Then he opened their minds to understand the scriptures, and said to them, "Thus it is written, that the Christ should suffer and on the third day rise from the dead, and that repentance and forgiveness of sins should be preached in his name to all nations, beginning from Jerusalem. You are witnesses of these things. And behold, I send the promise of my Father upon you; but stay in the city, until you are clothed with power from on high." (Luke 24:44-49, RSV)

When the Holy Spirit came in new power on the apostles at Pentecost, they began publicly to preach and teach what we must suppose to have been our Lord's own exposition to them of the Old Testament Scriptures. They preached as it were with Bible in hand. (See Acts 2:16 ff., 25 ff., 3:18, etc.) By this preaching they fulfilled the Lord's commission. "He commanded us to *preach* to the people" (Acts 10:42). The truth is that the apostolic preaching (the New

Testament in embryo) and the Old Testament Scriptures are inseparably interlocked, and are both ultimately inexplicable apart from each other.

A good example of the apostolic method, and the response which it both demanded and evoked, appears in the account of the preaching at Berea. The Bereans are commended by Luke as "more noble than those in Thessalonica" (Acts 17:11 f.) because they "received the word with all eagerness examining the (Old Testament) scriptures daily to see if these things were so," i.e., to test and verify the apostles' interpretation. Luke describes the total apostolic message—the Old Testament passages and their interpretation by the facts of Christ's life, death, resurrection, ascension, and the coming of the Spirit—as "the word," "the word of God" (vs. 13). It is through this word, preached or written, that faith comes, as it came to the Bereans (vs. 12). Through this word, humbly received and pondered by earnest minds, God begets saving faith in sinful men (Rom. 10:17).

So we conclude that the church never had any existence independent of the apostolic word of God. Like the individual convert, the church was begotten, as Peter says, of incorruptible seed "through the living and abiding word of God" (1 Pet. 1:23). Peter dwells on the fact that man and all man's glory are but as withering grass and fading flowers in comparison with the "word of the Lord" which "abides for ever." "And that word," Peter continues, "is the good news which was preached to you" (vss. 24 f.). Earlier in the chapter, Peter dovetails the gospel message into the Old Testament, as its fulfillment. Both have a common origin and author, he tells us; God by his Spirit, the Spirit of Christ, inspired both the prophets to foretell and the apostles to forth-tell (vss. 10 ff.), and the same Christ, crucified and glorified, was the burden of both their messages. It is this life-giving proclamation of Christ that creates the church through the new birth of individual believers. Then, as newborn babes, they grow through the milk of the word (1 Pet. 2:2; cf. 1 Cor. 3:2; Heb. 5:13). Thus it is as foolish to subordinate the word of God to the church as it would be to subordinate a mother to her baby, and to point to the latter as accounting for the existence of the former.

The Use of the Bible

We can only speak of "using" God's word in the same reverent sense in which we can think of "using" God. "Use" is really the wrong word here; for what the "using" in both cases amounts to is letting God have his way with us, bowing before him as he lays his hand on us. To "use" the Bible is not so much a matter of dealing with it as of having it deal with us. For the Bible is God's word, and God is the Great End, and men find life and salvation only in submission to him. Again, God the Holy Spirit is the true author and interpreter of the Scriptures, and we can only handle them to our profit if we do so in humble and reverent dependence on him for help. There is irreverence and irreligion inherent in any attitude towards Scripture, either in the church or in the individual, other than that of teachableness and submission. The attitude of submission does not imply any abdication of the powers of reason or private judgment, but, rather, it ensures their sanctification. It ensures that they will be used as they should be—not to sit in judgment on Scripture, but to judge the teaching of the church, and of individual teachers within the church, by the ultimate and decisive standards of the gospel word (Gal. 1:8; cf. 1 Cor. 15:3 f.).

Not, as we have seen, that this word can be separated from the Old Testament. "New" and "Old" cannot be divorced; they are inextricably bound together, as two parts of the same single message. Thus we may without violation of the apostle's mind apply to the whole Bible the words which Paul wrote to Timothy concerning the Old Testament: "All scripture is inspired by God, and is profitable for teaching, for reproof, for correction, and for training in righteousness, that the man of God may be complete, equipped for every good work" (2 Tim. 3:16 f.). As a verdict on the Old Testament, this is in very striking contrast with much that is said today. But Paul here assures Timothy that the Old Testament Scriptures, which had been the source of Timothy's instruction in childhood, and which were now fulfilled and completed by the word of the gospel, could still give him all that he needed as a leader of the church. Maturity, fullness of growth, and fitness for every duty as a man of God were to be realized through knowing and obeying those Scriptures. If Paul could speak thus of the Old Testament alone, how much more may his words be applied to the two Testaments taken together.

Paul continued with a solemn charge to Timothy— "Preach the word" (2 Tim. 4:2). Perilous times were coming for the church; evil teachers would arise; many would be led astray. The way of safety for Timothy, however, was to do the work of an evangelist, continuing in the things which he had learned— continuing, that is, in the path of scriptural and apostolic teaching. As Paul had reminded him earlier in the same letter, if he would be approved by God, a worker unashamed at Christ's coming, he must hold a straight course by unswerving fidelity to the divine word of the gospel and the Scriptures (see 2 Tim. 4:1-5; 2:15).

Paul's exhortations to Timothy in the Pastoral Epistles suggest to us a picture of the early church as a Bible-loving community. This, as we have seen, is in keeping with the church's origin in Judaism, our Lord's methods in his ministry, and the apostolic principles for evangelizing and edifying Jewish and Gentile converts. It appears also in the early church's worship. The small communities of Jewish and Gentile converts, as well as the wholly Jewish Christian groups in Jerusalem, which for a considerable period attended the Temple worship, perhaps until it ceased in 70 A.D., modelled their own distinctive meetings for Christian worship on the pattern of the synagogue (plus, of course, the added observance of the Lord's Supper and for a while the charismatic ministries of prophecy and tongues). The basic elements in the worship of the synagogue were Scripture readings, exhortations, praises, and prayers. The Scriptures were central; even today the Jewish synagogue has as its focal point the ark containing the sacred scrolls. Synagogue worship was directly founded on God's revelation of himself in the Scriptures. There the Old Testament was read and expounded, and the responses of praise and prayer were prompted and molded by the very thoughts and phrases of the written word. This was the background and model for early church worship. St. Paul, we note, commends, as worthy of special regard, the elders of the Christian congregation who, in addition to their tasks of pastoral care and discipline, ministered the word (1 Tim. 5:16); for this was, as it is still, the most honored form of ministry that the Christian presbyter can fulfill. No function in the church, clerical or lay, can supersede in importance the teaching of the Bible. We note too that among the special gifts which Paul discusses in 1 Corinthians 14 he ranks prophecy highest (next to the supreme gift of love, without which no other gift is valuable). He does so because prophecy—which must have included in those days inspired exposition of Old Testament Scriptures—ministers to edification, exhortation, and comfort (vss. 3, 22). In both 1 Corinthians 12:28 and Ephesians 4:11, prophets are placed next to apostles in the list of those gifted by the risen Christ to serve his church. This prophetic ministry is continued and exercised today in the exposition and application of the Scriptures of both Testaments. It is by this that the church lives and worships and increases.

How can we make the use of the Bible more effective in our own day? As compared with past generations, we have great advantages. Our people are literate, and Bibles in many good versions are cheap and easy to come by. But we have our disadvantages too. The Bible is no longer "*the* Book." The effect of the media is that people today are glutted with ideas from all quarters which, in ways that the parable of the Sower could never illustrate, may choke the seed of God's word. The printing presses turn out their floods of literature, good, bad, and indifferent. Radio and television hum with the spoken word and glitter with the living picture. Billboards and magazines shout their slogans. It seems impossible amid this welter of words and symbols to find entry for a message which speaks to the conscience and demands serious thought.

Should we not endeavor to capture all the media we can in order to "get across" the message of the Bible? In principle, our answer to this question must be: of course we should. Obvious possibilities at once suggest themselves. Parts of Scripture lend themselves to dramatization. Other parts can be enjoyed as great literature. But here we have to be on our guard lest by pandering to secular interests we misuse, and encourage others to misuse, the Bible. The Bible must not be set to serve the interests of dramatic effect or literary appreciation. For to start with, its real or supposed inadequacy in either of these spheres may lead to its being condemned and dismissed by people who have never heard it rightly used at all. And no one should be allowed as spectator or viewer to sit in judgment on the Bible as an entertainment; for the Bible is not an entertainment. It was never designed to amuse. It is the word of God; and every presentation or use of it must always bear witness to its divine authority, and be such as to express and create reverence for it and for its author. The Bible was not meant to be read as literature; some of its most important parts are poor as literary productions. Nor was it meant to provide scripts for dramatic entertainments; and to dramatize Scripture in such a way that the beholder is never shown his need for the evangelist who will point him through the wicket gate to the cross is to blunder. To film or televise the crucifixion story in a manner that awakens only horror and pity for Jesus is of little or no religious value, and might prove a real hindrance to a right understanding of the gospel, and of the mighty act of God on Calvary. Every right use of the Bible will respect and seek to realize the end for which it was all written.

What does this mean? It means that our approach to the Bible, social or personal, must be the approach of worship. Our use of Holy Scripture must take its place as part of our worship of God. The book which opens with "In the beginning, God . . ." and ends with "Come, Lord Jesus" can only be rightly handled on this level. The great themes of Scripture are prostituted if they become the mere passing cry of the disc jockey. The Bible can only be rightly used by those who fear God, or are willing to learn to fear God. The Bible can be used in the marketplace, but even there it must never be cheapened. Gospel wares are without money and without price because they are freely given to us through the sacrificial generosity of God; but they are in themselves of priceless worth, and must not be made to seem trivial and contemptible by the way in which we deal with the Book that proclaims them.

The title, "the *Holy* Bible," not only expresses the church's veneration for the sacred writings, but also indicates the only way in which Scripture can rightly be used. Our approach to it must be, not one of superstitious veneration for it as if it were a sort of charm, but one which reflects an awareness of the holiness of the God who speaks in the Bible, and of our own sinfulness and need to hear God's gracious words. For the Bible is not primarily a book for the speculative thinker, the scientific investigator, or the literary critic, but it is rather for the man who, having learned from the world around him and from his own heart something of God and of his own need, now seeks to know God and to find salvation.

It is for this reason that the Bible must always find its most proper and effective use in the worship and fellowship of the church, for it is there that the knowledge of God is sought and found. Those who conceive of the Bible as merely the message of God to the solitary individual are as superficial and unhistorical in their thinking as are those who would subordinate the Bible to the church on the grounds that the church existed first. The devout Christian will certainly spend much time in private with his Bible, but he will not forget that it is a book that has come to him through the life and witness of the people of

God; that all its roots are in the soil of ecclesiastical, churchly experience; and that only in such a context can it be adequately understood. The Bible cannot be taken seriously by the non-church-going individualist. Such a person is, by biblical standards, eccentric, off the center of Christianity.

Not, of course, that the Bible depends upon the church for its efficacy. Those who think otherwise are both unhistorical in their outlook and unspiritual also, for they limit the power of God. History has shown that the power of the Bible to speak to men is not in any way determined or delimited by the use, or misuse, to which the church officially puts it.

Our Lord promised to be in the midst of two or three gathered together in his name (Mt. 18:20). It is clear from the context that he is referring to a meeting of the local church, or Christian synagogue. In the first-century synagogue, worship was based on the acknowledgment of the Name of Jehovah as the one God, in a creed composed of Deuteronomy 6:4-9, 11:13-21, and Numbers 15:37-41, and it consisted, as we saw, in the reading of further Scriptures, exhortations, and the response of praise and prayer. What our Lord envisages here is the meeting of a Christian synagogue: for those who meet "in his name" are those who acknowledge him as Lord. The phrase "in my name" does not denote the mere repeating of the human name, Jesus, as if it were a spell or a talisman or a password, but the confessing of Jesus Christ as possessing the divine Name and nature and lordship (cf. Phil. 2:9-11). None, we are told, can confess that "Jesus is Lord" but by the enlightening and converting work of the Holy Spirit (1 Cor. 12:3). And Jesus is confessed as Lord "to the glory of God the Father" (Phil. 2:11)—his Father and ours. So Christian worship means the worship of God the Father as re-

vealed in and through Jesus Christ, the worship of
the God whose revealed Name—"Christian name," as
Barth sweetly called it—is Father, Son, and Holy
Ghost (Mt. 28:19 f.). It is when "two or three"—the
smallest possible number—meet together for the
purpose of this worship that the presence of the now
risen Christ is promised to them. The divine undertaking to hear and answer prayer that is offered
through the mediation of Christ supports and encourages the worshippers. "Almighty God," pray
those who use the Anglican form of Morning and
Evening Prayer, "who hast given us grace at this time
with one accord to make our common supplications
unto thee: and dost promise that when two or three
are gathered together in thy Name thou wilt grant
their requests . . ." (cf. Mt. 18:19 f.). The divine word
hallows and guides their devotion, confirming their
faith and building them up in the way of Christian
living. The divine Name is proclaimed, confessed,
and glorified, and the word itself is supreme
throughout.

The Lectionary

Let us now turn to the practical implications of this
position, which the Anglican Reformers drew out.
Cranmer, in the Preface to his first (1549) Prayer
Book, "Concerning the Service of the Church," wrote
of the "godly and decent order of the ancient
Fathers" in reading the whole Bible continuously
through each year. He sought to restore that godly
order by drawing up a Lectionary, which gave Scripture readings for two services every day. He based his
readings on the civil calendar, but followed ancient
custom in appointing the reading of particular books
for certain seasons, for instance Isaiah for Advent.
The main festivals had also appropriate passages, but

special occasional readings were kept down to a minimum, for Cranmer held that the continuous reading of books begun was a practice which must be maintained with as little interruption as possible. The reading of specially chosen portions as Epistles and Gospels at the Holy Communion provided the specific link with the liturgical emphasis of each particular Sunday. Cranmer's Preface, "The Order how the rest of Holy Scripture (except the Psalter) is appointed to be read," states his position clearly:

> The Old Testament is appointed for the first Lessons, at Matins and Evensong, and shall be read through every year once, except certain books and chapters, which be least edifying, and might best be spared, and therefore are left unread.

> The New Testament is appointed for the Second Lesson at Matins and Evensong, and shall be read over orderly every year thrice, beside the Epistles and Gospels; except the Apocalypse, out of which there be only certain lessons appointed upon divers feasts.

No church before or since has ever read the Bible so assiduously as Cranmer directed the Church of England to do.

Cranmer's basic plan of reading the whole Bible (a few passages excepted) year by year remained the foundation of the Anglican Lectionary till modern times, though more special lessons for festivals were appointed in the Calendar in subsequent revisions of the Prayer Book. Today, however, in face of the growing infrequency and irregularity of church attendance, the constant demand for shorter services, and the critical depreciation of many parts of Scripture, the idea of continuous and consecutive reading of the Bible as the basis of public worship has been largely abandoned. We have to ask ourselves:

can it be retained, even if in a less ambitious way than Cranmer and later revisers designed? or should we adopt the method, long in favor with Nonconformist bodies but now increasingly followed by others, of making the readings in each service a unity at the cost of ignoring the wider reach of revelation?

The position is further complicated for Anglicans by the growing practice of making the service of Holy Communion the main service of the Sunday, and teaching that it is the only one a Christian needs to come to. When this practice means using the Holy Communion service in isolation—something which the compilers of the Prayer Book never intended—and when it is taken as limiting the preacher to at most an abbreviated sermonette, in which no serious exposition of Scripture can be attempted, it has nothing to commend it. It is not primitive practice, it is not traditional Anglican practice, and it has no support from the New Testament church. As a way of using Scripture, it borders on the disastrous. It means, to start with, that the Old Testament is scarcely heard, save in some portions set for Epistles and in the reading of the Commandments, or the summary of the Law. To be sure, the Series 3 Alternative Service and lectionary provide for an Old Testament reading at each Communion Service, but in practice it is often omitted, perhaps more often than not. This naturally encourages a sort of practical Marcionism, in which the Old Testament is effectively ignored. The type of Christian produced by such means will be less informed and robust than an early church catechumen. Nor is this all. The isolation of the sacramental service from the systematic reading and exposition of the whole Bible will inevitably encourage a wrong view of the sacrament itself, and an unjustified and harmful disparagement of the other means of grace. There is no lack of present-day evidence that these are not neurotic Protestant fears; the thing is happening, all around us.

Whatever else may be attempted and authorized in lectionary revision, the continuous reading of the whole Bible to the whole congregation should not be forsaken. We recognize that the whole Bible cannot be covered at Sunday services in a single year; the two- and three-year cycles beloved of modern Anglican liturgists seem on inspection scarcely more adequate; a five- or even seven-year cycle would have been our own suggestion. It needs to be remembered that popular abbreviated services, even of Holy Communion, may achieve a kind of outward success which spells inward religious failure. The Low Mass of mediaeval Romanism held the people to a public acknowledgment of God which was in itself a breeding ground of superstition and religious perversion, because the corrective of systematic, balanced Scripture reading and instruction was absent. The continuous reading and preaching of the two Testaments provides the backbone and lifeblood for the church's worship, and there is no substitute for it. Without the virile and awe-inspiring truths of the Bible as the focus of attention, worship will be spineless, if not actually diseased and rotten. Prayers and praises not informed by scriptural truth and warmed by faith's grasp of the promises of grace remain cold, dry, and dead.

The great New Testament rubric for worship is that it must be in spirit and in truth (Jn. 4:24). It is remarkable that our Lord should have made this momentous declaration to a poor sinful woman in a wayside conversation. From this event, as from many other biblical passages, we learn that it is God's way and concern to bring ordinary men and women to himself by means of his own revealed instruction, and this should further confirm us in viewing and using the Scriptures of truth as the vehicle of grace in all our worship. There is, no doubt, a foolish bibliolatry which is as repugnant to true religion as is the relic worship of Rome; but there is also a true and proper veneration for God's written word, an attitude which realizes that to hear Holy Scriptures with reverence is the first step on the road to the purest worship of God. That written word, which came through the moving of men's hearts by the Holy Spirit, is still quick and powerful in its effect upon those who hear it (see 2 Pet. 1:21; Heb. 4:12). By it, God awakens, enlightens, and heals, and then stirs men up to the most ardent and truly spiritual devotion. The rubrical direction before the reading of the lessons in Morning and Evening Prayer, that they shall be read "distinctly with an audible voice," the reader "so turning himself, as he may best be heard of all such as are present," is not merely a reminder that church acoustics are often bad; it is primarily a summons to a reverent and expectant attitude towards the Scripture on the part of both reader and people. We may compare the custom, retained in our service of Holy Communion, of standing for the reading of the gospel. This, too, is a mark of expectant reverence for the words of Christ himself, which the congregation is about to hear. Where God's word is read, there God is speaking to man, and such a place is holy ground.

Once it is realized that the mainspring of worship is God's disclosure of his Name by his word, the current controversy about the focal point in church architecture and the relative importance of articles of church furniture may speedily be settled. The focal point is where God's word is read or taught. Pagan spies at early Christian services reported that they had no object of worship—there was no visible focal point. Later, though before the development of ornate buildings in the fourth century, the seat of the presiding presbyter or bishop became the central object in the church. Why? Because from it God's word was taught. At this period a small moveable wooden table was all that was used for Communion services. The truth is that the focal point in a church building is to be found by the ear, as well as the eye. It is the place from which God speaks, that is, the place from which his word is heard. This dictates a prominent place for the lectern and pulpit, at least as prominent as the place given to the Communion Table. There is no justification for a relative disparagement of either word or sacrament; both must be recognized as means of the selfsame grace given through the one gospel, and the arrangement of our churches ought to reflect that recognition.

The Pulpit

The Bible, we have said, is the word of God. In it God speaks, and to it we must listen. Listening to it, through the witness of the Spirit of Christ in and through the prophets and apostles, we hear Christ himself. To enthrone this biblically recorded testimony to Christ as the rule of Christian faith and life is to be in the true apostolic succession. The inspired witness of prophets and apostles must always govern the Church, and faithful preachers of each generation must subordinate themselves to it. We shall now consider the place of preaching as a vehicle of the word of God.

If by preaching we mean mere oratory or talking about religion in a way that is not biblically inspired or informed, let us be clear that such preaching is neither a means of grace nor a proper part of worship. As a use of the voice, it may be entertaining and informative, but saving and sanctifying it cannot be. The use of the Bible in the pulpit is the necessary condition of true Christian preaching. Nonbiblical preaching, mere religious lecturing for the diffusion of the speaker's private ideas, has no place in Christian worship. Preaching, if not sacramental, is profane. By this we mean that a true sermon is an act of God, and not a mere performance by man. In real preaching the speaker is the servant of the word and God speaks and works by the word through his servant's lips. There is no conflict or rivalry between genuine preaching and the ministry of the sacraments: both are proclamations of the same message, and God works through both to the same effect. Often, indeed, when the pulpit has lapsed from faithful proclamation of the word a scriptural sacramental liturgy has conserved gospel truth for the people. In their essential simplicity the sacraments are anchored fast to the saving facts of the faith, and we may be sure that the Holy Communion service has kept near to the heart of the gospel multitudes who would have been far from divine grace if their spiritual health had depended on the pulpit ministrations that they received. On the other hand, however, we cannot forget the plain lesson of pre-Reformation history, that the sacraments, especially if not ministered simply in the common tongue in the context of biblical preaching, can become dumb ceremonies and magical rites, breeding grounds for blasphemy and superstition. From this point of view, we must insist that the right use of the Bible in the pulpit is a necessary safeguard for the due administration of the sacraments.

Perhaps the greatest need of the church today is

that clergy and laity should recover a true understanding of the function of the sermon. The sermon is an integral part of worship. It is God's ordained means of speaking and working. The divine commission to ministers is a commission to preach and teach, and the accompanying promise is that, if they preach the word faithfully, they will not preach in vain. What they say must come from Scripture, or be demonstrably "agreeable to the same," and men must hear it with reverence as the means of their salvation. Great heights of adoration, praise, and worship can be reached by a devout congregation during the sermon, as the things of God pass before them. Souls are saved and filled with the Holy Spirit as the word is preached. Victories in the spiritual life of far-reaching personal and social consequences may be won under the power of the sermon. The Anglican liturgy, with its high biblical standard and content, requires good biblical preaching to match its lofty spiritual tone. A sermon in which the Bible is not rightly used makes a sad anticlimax to a service in which Holy Scripture has determined the entire outlook and provided all the dominant themes until the preacher began.

It would be a good thing if every congregation could periodically witness a Prayer Book Ordination service, and observe the dramatic simplicity of the delivering of the Bible as the symbol and instrument of the minister's authority and commission. It is a useful discipline for every clergyman to read often through this same service, so as to keep fresh and clear before his mind the high demands of his calling as a minister of the word. The Church of England is most explicit in stating what the right use of the Bible in the pulpit must involve in the private lives of its clergy, and this is something which both clergy and laity need to appreciate. Let us note what the Ordinal says about it.

In the Ordering of Priests, in the exhortation before the questions which precede the laying on of hands, the Bishop reminds the candidates that the only way in which they can fulfill their weighty responsibility of caring for the souls of men is by daily study of the Scriptures. All worldly cares and studies must be set aside, so that adequate time may be given to "reading and learning the scriptures." By such a course of "daily reading and weighing of the scriptures," they may hope to "wax riper and stronger" in their ministry. The Ordinal clearly implies that the secret of an effective ministry is to know and use the Bible. The solemn delivery of the Bible, as the seal of authority to preach the word and minister the sacraments, focuses the teaching of the service on this matter. Then, in the prayer which follows, the thought of God's heavenly blessing upon the ministry of those ordained is interpreted by the petitions—"that thy Word spoken by their mouths may have such success, that it may never be spoken in vain"; "grant also, that we may have grace to hear and receive what they shall deliver out of thy most holy Word, or agreeable to the same, as the means of our salvation." This is the criterion of successful ministry, according to the Ordinal—that a man should be a faithful and effective communicator of the biblical message.

The Ordinal makes it plain that a pulpit ministry which is to be successful in this way will depend upon the diligent, prayerful study of the Scriptures. Such success is not cheaply or easily obtained, or else it would be more common than it is. The price has to be paid in daily study and toil. Yet what is there more satisfying or rewarding than the consciousness, sometimes in God's goodness vividly bestowed, that a congregation is by grace receiving the word preached as truly the word of God and the means of salvation? In our day, when the clergy are often busy about many things, there is all the greater need to guard the time which must be given "to the word of God and prayer" (Acts 6:4). Use of the Bible in the study will drive a man to his knees, and the treasures of the book, the things new and old that break upon his view will be a never-failing source of freshness and inspiration to him in his spiritual life. And they will also be the wellspring of worthy pulpit success.

It is not our task here to outline methods of Bible study, a subject on which many excellent books have been written. We would, however, emphasize that the basic requirement in any scheme of private reading for clergy or laity, no less than in a lectionary for public use, is the continuous reading of the entire Scriptures. The Anglican provision of daily offices at least for the clergy, and the obligation thereby imposed upon them to read consecutively the lessons set from both Testaments, is worthy of note in this connection. While each individual will have his own favorite pastures in Holy Writ, the minister must be constantly careful to see that he delivers the whole counsel of God in his teaching, and this he can best do by following not only the Prayer Book system of reading the whole Bible, but also the lead given by its actual choice of lessons—that is, by expounding from the various parts of Scripture, as set in the lectionary. This kind of biblical preaching, set in the structure of the main festivals of the Christian year, will provide not only a full-orbed presentation of the gospel, but also a wholesome corrective to narrow views of revelation. Much of the anemic and lopsided religion found in churches which do not use a liturgy nor attempt to read the whole Bible in public worship has

arisen through allowing the personal likes and dis-
likes of the minister to dictate how the Bible is used.

If the whole Bible is not only read at the lectern,
but used as the basis and authority for pulpit
teaching, it will soon invade the pew. Bible preaching
demands, and will create, Bible-reading, Bible-using
congregations. Anglicanism assumes that its members at their best will be like the Bereans, able and
active to judge and assess whether the teaching they
hear is in accordance with Scripture (see Article Six).
In former generations, the Bible and Prayer Book
bound up in one volume were in regular use.
Another popular volume contained the Prayer Book
and the set lessons. We wonder how many of those
who are pessimistic about the possibility today of
seeing Bible-reading congregations listening to biblical, doctrinal sermons have ever seriously tried to
produce such a phenomenon. Those who have tried
have not found the undertaking so hopeless as some
might imagine. What has been, can be, and, thank
God, in many places is. The necessary machinery is
put within the grasp of all of us in the Prayer Book
services, with the lectionary and the set Gospels and
Epistles. It is true, indeed, that failure and ineffec-
tiveness have marked the modern church wherever it
has tried more superficial methods; nor need we
wonder at this, for little grace can be expected where
the great means of grace is neglected. We believe that
many ministers could profitably cut out many week-
day activities which interfere with their time for
study of God's word, and work to greater effect
through the consequent enrichment of their
preaching and teaching. If we do not succeed in the
services of public worship on the Lord's Day, our
ministry fails miserably. Let our self-assessment begin there.

But, it is said, the age of preaching is past. The problems of communicating the faith in our secular society make it impossible for the pulpit to have the power today that it used to have. Frankly, we refuse to believe it. Much nonsense is talked these days about the problems of communication. The problems of communication are basically no different from what they always have been, and the old solution of them remains valid. It still remains true that, though "the natural man receiveth not the things of the Spirit of God: for they are foolishness unto him" (1 Cor. 2:14), those that are of the truth will hear the word of Christ. He calls his sheep, and they know him, and follow him, and learn to distinguish his voice from that of the stranger (Jn. 10:4 f.). We can magnify the problems of our age to such an extent as virtually to deny the ministry of the Holy Spirit, as the inspirer of Scripture who interprets it in the life of the church. There is a pessimism which produces paralysis, and is first cousin to unbelief. We do well to remember the words of Rabbi Duncan to the young man who persisted in adding his comments when he read the Scriptures in public: "Young man, let the Holy Ghost speak!" The New Testament church commenced without prestige, or patronage, or learning of the schools; all that the first Christians had was the word of God and the Holy Spirit; and they turned the world upside down. What do we lack that they had? Let our self-assessment continue.

The Use of the Bible in Pastoral Work

It would be a mistake to think that the life of the church depends only on the use of the Bible in the pulpit, although, as we have seen, it depends a great deal on that. But the minister who is faithful in using the Bible there will appreciate the need to use it everywhere in his pastoral ministry. Pastoring means preaching, but it means more than preaching. Much of the ministry of the apostles was exercised informally to small groups and from house to house. Following the Master's example, they spoke the word both in the marketplace and in the home: which is still the proper way. The Church of England Ordinal asks would-be presbyters: "Will you be ready, with all faithful diligence, to banish and drive away all erroneous and strange doctrines contrary to God's Word; and to use both public and private monitions and exhortations, as well to the sick as to the whole, within your cures, as need shall require, and occasion shall be given?" Here is required faithful ministry to the individual, with Bible in hand, teaching, correcting, admonishing, comforting—doing, in fact, those very things for which Paul says that the Holy Scriptures are profitable (2 Tim. 3:15 ff.). Two aspects of this ministry may be specially noted.

First: the way to fulfill a pastoral ministry towards the *young and adolescent* is outlined in the Catechism. In former days, with smaller communities, the parson in person would do as the rubrics of the Catechism require, and catechize the young in the presence of the congregation. This was not intended as a substitute for home instruction, but an adjunct to it. The children would be with their parents in church, so that they might "hear sermons" from Scripture, as the Exhortation which ends the Baptismal Service requires. For some generations now, however, the Sunday School has been taking the place of catechetical teaching in public worship, and it is often taken for granted that the minister is too busy looking after the adults to do more than pay an occasional visit to the juvenile department and, perhaps, arrange a special service for the children every now and then. But with the present decay and decline of Sunday Schools, the whole situation needs to be re-examined.

In the early days, when Sunday Schools virtually did duty for the then non-existent day schools, they were successful. In those days they offered, not simply religious instruction, but an all-round elementary education for the nonprivileged. Today, however, with education so largely secularized, non-church-going parents the rule, and the Bible neither known nor bothered with, the Sunday Schools are failing and losing their grip on the situation. What is to be done? We believe that the answer in most parishes lies in a reacceptance by the clergy of a major share in teaching the young, or at any rate the adolescent groups; and, with this, a greater stress on parental responsibility in connection with the religious instruction of children. Those who clamor for the early confirmation of children before teen-age as a means of grace to them would be more in accord with Scripture if they gave greater diligence to teaching the young the Bible. This, rather than childhood communion, is the great means of grace to fortify young people against the storms of adolescence. "From childhood," wrote Paul to Timothy, "you have been acquainted with the sacred writings which are able to instruct you for salvation" (2 Tim. 3:15). Paul appeals to this foundation of biblical knowledge, a foundation laid in childhood, to fortify young Timothy against the coming apostasy. Timothy's teachers had been first his mother and grandmother and then, in young manhood, the apostle himself. Here, surely, is the ideal combination in religious training—the parents, the earliest and most constant teachers, beginning, and the minister, the occasional and specialized teacher, working with them. The divine commandment to the Hebrew parent to teach the truths of God to his children at all times (Dt. 6:7) is enforced in the New Testament (Eph. 6:4), and no passage of time or altered circumstances can make obsolete this biblical pattern, which makes the home the sanctuary of the faith.

So to our second theme: pastoral ministry *in the home*.

Can we reestablish the use of the Bible in the homes of Christian people? Can we revive the practice of family worship and instruction? One thing, at least, is certain: the place which the clergy give to the Bible in the church, and in teaching the young and old, and the pattern of the pastoral ministry which they fulfill in their people's homes, will soon be reflected, for better or for worse, in the conduct of family life by the members of their congregations. What sort of ministry in the home should Anglican clergy be fulfilling? The Ordinal envisages a pastoral ministry, with the Bible in hand, directed both to the sick and to the whole. Visiting, therefore, must have a specific spiritual intention—to teach, or exhort, or comfort and encourage, or to evangelize. The pastor whose calls are regularly associated with the reading of the Scriptures and prayer leaves an impression on the life of the family which paves the way for the introduction of family devotions. A simple service of reading and prayer at the bedside of an invalid, if possible with the whole family present, may seem old-fashioned and unusual, but it is unrivalled in its impact and effects. The old service for the Visitation of the Sick may not be convenient for use today, but attention to the emphases of its prayers and rubrics would redeem much sick visiting from superficiality and ineptness. The suggested list of Scripture readings added to the service in the proposed English

Prayer Book of 1928 was possibly the best thing in that ill-fated revision.

The compiling of a list of suitable passages for a specific pastoral use is not, of course, new. It is a practice implicit in many Prayer Book passages. In one realm of pastoral work it is of special value, namely in dealing with burdened penitents. The Prayer Book shows itself vividly aware of this. The sentences at the opening of Morning and Evening Prayer are chosen specially to arouse and comfort the sinful; the Comfortable Words in the Holy Communion service are of particular value for bringing assurance of forgiveness; and the long catena of passages in the second part of the Exhortation in the Commination service is unrivalled as a statement of God's free and gracious pardon.

It is, indeed, implied in the Exhortations on the need for due preparation before receiving the sacrament of the Lord's Supper that lay people in the Church of England will, in the words of Hooker, "know how to heal their own wounds." They will be familiar with the promises of God, and able to exercise faith in them. That in itself, of course, presupposes a gospel-preaching, Bible-teaching ministry and a Bible-reading people. But even so it is recognized that some in spiritual need may be unable to quiet their consciences. The first Exhortation urges such a one to go to his parish clergyman, "or to some other learned and discreet Minister of God's Word, and open his grief." The pastor will then bring him "by the ministry of God's holy Word . . . the benefit of absolution, together with ghostly [spiritual] counsel and advice." The nature of this absolution may be gathered from the context. It is the absolution given "by the ministry of God's holy Word." It is, in other words, a particular exercise of the "power and commandment" given by our Lord to his ministers to "declare and pronounce" to his penitent, believing people the reality of the remission of their sins. (See the Prayer of Absolution in Morning and Evening Prayer.) This ministry of absolution is to be exercised toward the individual by a skillful and gracious use of the Bible, in the name of its Author, for this most sacred of all tasks, the restoring and healing of the penitent sinner. The Order for the Visitation of the Sick envisages a similar ministry at all times, and for exceptional cases where a sick man, troubled in conscience, has made "a special confession of his sins" and now desires confirmatory assurance of his pardon, it provides an indicative form of absolution for the minister to use.

In view of the widespread use of the confessional in various forms, and the arguments from alleged pastoral expediency which are commonly put forward to justify such use, it is worth pausing once more to stress the view of the place and function of the Bible which underlies this and all Prayer Book teaching. The Prayer Book assumes that the ordinary ministrations of the church will create Christians who are "alive to God" and know for themselves the way of peace with him. Such will normally be able to "heal their own wounds" by applying the gospel promises to themselves in private acts of faith and repentance. In exceptional circumstances and emergencies, some may need special treatment, but such cases are seen as abnormal, and the aim of the treatment will be to bring them to the point where they need special treatment no longer. Anything like the confessional would only ever be needed in times of spiritual sickness; in terms of the Prayer Book outlook, it could never be thought of as an accompaniment or precondition of normal spiritual health.

The Devotional Use of the Bible

In this last section of our discussion, we propose to
consider the use of the Bible in personal communion
with God. The Church of England, as we have seen,
thinks of the normal spiritual life as one of constant
fellowship with God, in full enjoyment of the peace
which the assurance of his love and mercy brings.
What part does the use of the Bible play in bringing
about and maintaining this state? Turn again to our
unrivalled Prayer Book. We shall find in its use of the
Bible in prayer and praise the true pathway of personal religion.

We observe first the Collect for the Second Sunday
in Advent, which sums up in a sentence the Reformers' whole attitude and approach to Scripture, and
breathes the spirit which animated their own devotional use of it.

> Blessed Lord, who hast caused all holy scriptures to
> be written for our learning: Grant that we may in such
> wise hear them, read, mark, learn, and inwardly digest
> them, that by patience and comfort of thy holy Word, we
> may embrace and ever hold fast the blessed hope of
> everlasting life, which thou hast given us in our Saviour
> Jesus Christ.

The Collect may have been Archbishop Cranmer's
own composition. It filled a gap which existed in the
collects taken over from the older service books. It
was true, indeed, that Scripture had inspired the
form and content of the ancient collects, as it did the
newer compositions of the Reformers. But now this
further collect was added, stating explicitly, in the
form of address, the end for which God had provided
Scripture and, in the form of petition, the proper use

and fruit of the Bible in the spiritual life.

A noticeable feature of this collect is its direct relationship to the Epistle which follows it (Rom. 15:4-13). It is the message of the Epistle distilled into prayer. The ancient collects, apart from later corruptions, had usually been based on Scripture, but not necessarily on the Epistle or Gospel for the Day. Cranmer and his associates, however, here make the desirable link between Scripture and prayer explicit and patent. The prayers that are offered by the faithful are to be based upon the Scriptures that they read. This gives us the clue at once to the right use of the Bible in the devotional life. God's word comes to us so that we may then speak our word to him. Union and communion with God, and abiding in Christ, is the great end of all true religion, and it is brought about by God's own gracious activity. God approaches man in and by his word, disclosing himself there; the worshipper takes that word of revelation and turns it into prayer, praise, and adoration as he approaches God. Christian prayer is never blind groping and haphazard speaking, but is always in essence intelligent response to God's word in Scripture.

This basic fact about the Christian life, which is so clearly taught and expressed in all Prayer Book worship, sets the pattern for our use of the Bible in private devotion and study. Public worship and exposition, and private Bible reading and prayer, are interrelated. An intelligent, spiritual use of the Bible by the individual should be fostered and directed by the way in which he hears the Bible used in the prayer desk, at the lectern, and in the pulpit. Misuse of the Bible here will have unfavorable repercussions there. Conversely, the achievement of those whose duty it is to lead public worship will depend very much on the way in which they use the Bible in private. The quality and vitality of men's preaching and praying (particularly when their prayers are extempore, or personally composed) will vary according to the reality or otherwise of their life of personal devotion. Praise and prayer soon dry up, or become formal, flat and anemic, if they are not deeply and freshly nourished by the Word of God.

The opening words of the Collect show us another important fact. God has caused *all* Holy Scripture to be written for our learning. As in the life of the Church, so in the life of the individual, the whole Bible must be used. We are all prone to fall into the trap of reading only our own favorite passages or books, which may lead to serious consequences, both in distorted views of God and in unbalanced spiritual development, and we must watch ourselves here. It may, for instance, be a comforting thing to have a box packed with the promises of Holy Scripture, which you can draw out at random when you feel you need some inspiration. But ought we not to have a precept box, or even a threat box, beside our promise box to counterbalance this rather doubtful way of using God's word? In any case boxed texts cannot set before us anything like the sweep of Scripture. Similarly, *Daily Light* has no doubt brought help to all of us at times, but it is none the less a dangerous substitute for reading the Bible. Just as there are congregations which hear much of an edited version of the Sermon on the Mount and little or nothing of the Ten Commandments, so there are individual Christians whose diet of Scripture is restricted to a few chosen Psalms and the Gospels. There is, we may be sure, more in any one of these parts of Holy Writ than we shall ever fathom, but we are less likely to make headway in understanding them rightly if we isolate them from the rest of God's revelation.

When we stress the need to read the whole Bible continually, we do not imply that mere reading is sufficient in itself. Concentrated thought and prayerful application are required too. The Collect which we are using to illustrate the personal use of the Scriptures is itself an example of this, in the way that it distils the teaching and thrust of the Epistle (Rom. 15:4-13) which it precedes.

Let us hear again the instruction embodied in the Collect's central petition, "Grant that we may in such wise *hear* them, *read, mark, learn,* and *inwardly digest* them, that . . . we may embrace, and ever hold fast the blessed hope of everlasting life . . .".

Hear, says the Collect. How you hear is as important as what you hear. "If any man has ears to hear, let him hear," said our Lord. In the sixteenth century, as in our Lord's day, many could not read, and hearing was their only means of coming to understand. But speaking is still the primary mode of communication in the church, so that it is still very largely true that salvation depends upon hearing well. No doubt more souls are lost through bad hearing than through bad preaching or bad reading. We must pay the word of God most reverent attention.

And we must do more. We who are literate ought to *read* Scripture as well as hear it, and furthermore we must *mark* it, and *learn* it, and *inwardly digest* it. There is a progression of intensity in application implied by the language here. We are to read God's word so often and so diligently that we know it, and have it hidden securely in our memory. Also we are to turn it over in our minds, taking note of it and assimilating it into our moral and spiritual system, so that it dwells in our hearts and becomes part of us, as our food does. Learning by rote has gone out of fashion, but it is doubtful whether we can afford to do without it; there is certainly no substitute for an intimate familiarity with what is in the Bible. Bishop Ridley's moving words of farewell to the Cambridge college where he had lived as student and master reveal the passionate practical love of God's word which possessed the fathers of the reformed English church.

> Farewell, Pembroke Hall, of late mine own college, my cure and my charge. In thy orchard (the walls, butts, and trees, if they could speak, would bear me witness) I learned without book almost all Paul's epistles, yea and I ween all the canonical epistles, save only the Apocalypse. Of which study, although in time a great part did depart from me, yet the sweet smell thereof I trust I shall carry into heaven; for the profit thereof I think I have felt in all my life time ever after.

The constant use of the Psalter in the services of the church has printed much of it upon the memory of God's children, and it is good that this should be so. The Psalter is the hymn book and prayer book of the Old Testament. The heights of spiritual understanding and experience which many of its writers reached reveal the richness of devotional life which the saints of God could know even before the coming of Christ. And although the Christian has the fuller and more complete revelation, he can still use—indeed, he cannot do better than use—as the vehicle of his aspiration and devotion the words in which the Psalmists speak to and of God out of their own full hearts. Psalm 119 is perhaps the richest treasury that the church has ever possessed on the faithful man's use of the word of God. While the Psalmist does not actually use the metaphor of digestion to illustrate the believer's assimilation of God's truth, he does write of it as his own most delectable food. God's words, he says, are sweeter than honey in his mouth (verse 103). He has a longing for God's commandments that is like physical hunger and thirst (verses 123, 131). His greatest wealth, above fine gold, is the rich treasure of God's law (verse 127). This is so, because God himself is his portion, his possession, through his allegiance to God's word (verse 57). Therefore he makes God's law the object of his meditation all the day long and even through the night (verses 97, 148).

In the New Testament, Christ and the apostles underline in a remarkable way this view of the relations of the word of God and the man of God to each other. Christ's word cleanses (Jn. 15:3); it is to dwell in us (vs. 7), and we are to abide in it (Jn. 8:31). John teaches that Christ's word cannot be in us if we do not acknowledge our sins and seek cleansing (1 Jn. 1:10); but if we keep Christ's commandments, that is evidence that we know him, and proof that we abide in him, and he in us (1 Jn. 2:3, 3:24). We cannot separate either Christ or Christian experience from the Bible. Our attitude to the written word decisively affects our relationship to the living word. The secret of spiritual fullness is to let the word of Christ dwell in us in all its intrinsic richness (Col. 3:16). Like Jeremiah of old, we should eat it (Jer. 15:16); we should set ourselves to live on it, and live by it.

Meditation, the mental and spiritual counterpart of digestion, is the most important exercise of all in our use of the Bible. Meditation is not giving free rein to your imagination, nor is it reading your Bible for beautiful thoughts. Meditation is a discipline. It starts and continues with Scripture itself. Reason and imagination are called into play, not to run free and create, but to probe and to understand. In meditation, the whole man is engaged in deep and prayerful thought on the true meaning and bearing of a particular biblical passage, on its revelation of God and his ways with men, and on its application to our own life. Nor are we left to ourselves in this. The divine Author of Scripture is not dead. Again the Psalmist comes to our help and gives us the appropriate words to use as we turn to the Bible—"open my eyes, that I may behold wondrous things out of thy law" (Ps. 119:18). How often must Paul have prayed in such terms for his Christian hearers and readers, that God would open the eyes of their understanding (cf. Eph. 1:17)—not that they might have visions of truths hitherto unrevealed, but that they might know, with the deep, transforming knowledge that inward digestion gives, the glory of the things which Paul himself proclaimed, the things set forth in the gospel of our Lord Jesus Christ. To this end are we to meditate, in this spirit of dependence, and within these stated limits. To be useful to our souls, meditation must be anchored to the word of God. We do not follow cunningly devised fables when we commit ourselves to the apostles' message (2 Pet. 1:16), and we cannot and need not go beyond their witness to Christ. God may, indeed, have more light to break from his holy word, but let us be careful that what we receive as light does in fact come from his word, and not from the false fires of our own fancy.

The minister who is to preach biblically can only do so as a result of much meditation. He must live with a passage until God makes it live to him; only then can he make it live to his people. It is only out of this experience that a man can enter the pulpit with a sense upon him of having a message from God for his hearers. Other skills are involved in preaching, but this is the spring and birthplace of the dynamic use of Scripture in the pulpit. For this, above all, the preacher needs to pray; and his people too. De Witt

Talmadge, an American preacher of the last century, once said that poor preaching was God's curse on a prayerless parish. How important it is that the minister's sermon preparation, his seeking for light and for a door of utterance, should be aided by the prayers of his flock.

There is a warning against misuse of the Bible which our Reformers, following the Fathers, found it necessary to issue and reiterate, and we do well to heed it again in our own day. In his preface to the English Bible of 1540, Cranmer says that he is writing chiefly for two sorts of people, those who need the spur and those who need the bridle. The spur is for those who are too slow, the bridle for those who are too quick. "In the latter sort," he writes, "be they, which by their inordinate reading, undiscreet speaking, contentious disputing, or otherwise, by their licentious living, slander and hinder the word of God most of all other, whereof they seem to be the greatest furtherers." He quotes Gregory of Nazianzus, who found it necessary to speak against such people in his day as men with the tongue itch, whose whole delight was to talk and chatter. All their holiness consisted in talking. They could excuse each other from upright living so long as they stayed together in their argumentation. It was a tragedy for the cause of true religion that the Reformation movement was so soon infected with this kind of conceited and rancorous wrangling. In 1582, the anonymous publisher of Cranmer's pungent comments on the supposed "unwritten verities" of the church of Rome complained bitterly of talkers on the Bible who were not walkers with God. We today must mourn the continuance of this unholy use of the Bible. There have always been men who would fight and argue about the Bible and for the Bible with zeal enough and to spare, but in a loveless, repellent and disruptive manner, God can and will defend his word by means of weapons fashioned from it, but those who would wield such weapons must themselves be living epistles of the grace of God (cf. 2 Cor. 3:2 f.). After all, even the devil can quote Scripture for his own ends, and he will be quick to exploit any ungodly use of it by men. A loveless handling of the Bible is but a means of discord, not of edification in love; it is like sounding brass, or a tinkling cymbal. We need to beware of vain and bitter wranglings, and "strife about words" (cf. 2 Tim. 2:14). The form of sound words, received from the apostles of Christ, can only be held effectively and religiously when it is held "in the faith and love which are in Christ Jesus" (2 Tim. 1:13). No one can rightly use the Bible who is not seeking and serving Christ, nor abiding in the love of God, nor pursuing wisdom and holiness.

Our final word, gathering everything together, must be this: that the Christian's use of the Bible must correspond with Christ's own use of the Bible. For, to quote some words of Bishop Handley Moule,

> He, in the days of his flesh, was the supreme Bible student, the supreme lover, employer, and expositor of the Bible. Look again at the fact as it stands out in the four Gospels. See "this same Jesus" as he upheld Himself and foiled the enemy with the Bible in the Temptation, as He opened His message with it at Nazareth, as He quoted its syllables twice over on the Cross. Walk to Emmaus with Him, and see Him spending the whole Easter afternoon upon the Bible. He had come that morning from the grave, conqueror of death, Lord of life, and He came as it were with the Bible in his hands.

He trampled upon many popular opinions of his day, where he thought they needed correction, but he did not trample upon the universal Jewish belief that the

Bible was divine, the written word of God, declaring God's truth and imbued with God's authority. No, *that* belief he sanctioned and sanctified. And it is for us to treat the Bible as he did. We need not fear to approach it: no lack of intellectual power, real or fancied, need hinder us from knowing God through it, for, as Jesus taught, it is the Father s way to hide his truth from the clever and conceited, and to reveal it, and himself with it, to babes (Mt. 11:25). Let us, then, take our Bibles afresh and resolve by God's grace henceforth to make full use of them. Let us read them with reverence and humility, seeking the illumination of the Holy Spirit. Let us meditate on them till our sight is clear and our souls are fed. Let us live in obedience to God's will as we find it revealed to us in Scripture; and the Bible will prove itself both a lamp to our feet and a light upon our path. May it please the divine Author of Holy Scripture to give to us and to all his people that for which the Litany asks: "increase of grace, to hear meekly (his) Word, and to receive it with pure affection, and to bring forth the fruits of the Spirit." For that will be life indeed.

CHAPTER FOUR

The Bible and the Church

"They lived happily ever after." So say fairy tales of imaginary married couples, and so wrote middle-aged Winston Churchill in the closing sentence of *My Early Life* about his own marriage with Clementine Hosier. I take him to have been telling the world two things. The first, which is there on the surface, is that they had become consciously inseparable, and the bond between them was growing stronger all the time. The second, which human nature makes certain though it was not stated, is that they had had ups and downs ("Christian rows," as a clergyman friend once prettily put it), and would doubtless have more, but had reached the point of knowing that their relationship would survive the rows and not be destroyed by them. But the fairy-tale phrase does not hint at this, nor at the inner complexity of the marriage relationship from any standpoint at all; that knowledge is supplied by experience. Something similar is true of the relation between the Bible and the church. The Bible is and always has been the book of the church, the source of its faith, thought, preaching, teaching, order, worship, praise, prayer, song. The inseparability is conscious; the church always has been, and when in its senses has tried to show itself to be, the people of the book, learning its identity, calling, mission, knowledge of God and knowledge of itself in and under God, from the pages of Holy Writ. Bunyan's pilgrim with his book in his hand could be a picture of the church no less than of the Christian. But this is not the whole story. The relation between Bible and church has so varied in different periods and in different theologies that accusations of destroying it have often been heard within the church's own ranks, as in some places they are heard today. Also, though the relation may be simple and straightforward in idea, it regularly proves tense and complex in practice, just because Bible and church are both intrinsically complex realities. Our first step in approaching our theme, therefore, had better be to warn ourselves against oversimplifying.

A glance at history gives perspective. The first major debate on Bible-church relations took place at the Reformation, when Roman and anti-Roman began to accuse each other of laying waste the church through misunderstanding Scripture. Up till then Christians had been taught to assume the identity of the church's religion with the biblical faith, and any who did not were categorized as heretical monsters. The Reformers queried this identity at a deep level. They accused Rome of contradicting Scripture over the mediation of Christ, the work of the Spirit, the way of salvation, the method of grace, the meaning of justification and faith, the doctrine and use of the sacraments, especially the Lord's Supper, and the nature of the church itself; also, they diagnosed the Roman appeal to tradition as binding and gagging the Bible so that it could not speak and be heard. For saying this the Reformers were, to be sure, categorized as heretical monsters, but they made their point at least to this extent, that they compelled Rome to argue for her position and to recognize that it could no longer be taken for granted.

In that debate the main issues were the *extent, clarity,* and *sufficiency* of Scripture. On the first issue Rome said: the canon of Scripture is known through the church's decision, which when conciliar is infallible (as when the Council of Trent defined the Old Testament apocrypha into the canon, something never before done). Protestants said: the authority of church use and definition though weighty is not final nor divine, and recognition of canonical Scripture depends ultimately on the covenanted inner witness of the Spirit, whereby the divine source and authority of those books which the church has historically attested (not, therefore, the apocrypha) is made evident to faith. On the second issue, Rome said: Scripture is not self-explanatory, and the Bible reader who does not let the teaching church tell him what the book means will err to his soul's hurt. Protestants said: though it is true that God has appointed the preaching of the word as the prime means of Christian understanding, yet all things necessary to salvation are plain in the biblical text, so that he who reads attentively, seeking the Spirit's help and comparing Scripture with Scripture, will not be led astray. On the third issue Rome said: Scripture needs to be supplemented by traditions which the church hands down. Protestants replied: the absence of traditional items (papacy, penances, pilgrimages, what have you) from the Bible argues their nonnecessity and probable unsoundness. Urged the Reformers: the basic form of the church's discipleship to its Lord is to echo Scripture in its confession and obey Scripture in its life, changing its present ways in whatever way Scripture proves to require. Replied Rome: the church serves its Lord most truly by transmitting the whole deposit of faith and moral teaching found within its tradition, of which Scripture is only part. The debate has continued.

But within Protestantism things were complicated by the progressive outworking of two Renaissance motifs, man's intellectual autonomy and his status as the measure of all things. These soon dissolved the frame of reference within which the Reformation debate took place. Both Rome and the Reformers were clear that this world depends on a Creator who rules and speaks, who governs its whole course and makes miraculous redemptive intrusions into it, and that both church and Bible are products of such intrusion, the former through regeneration, the latter by inspiration. But seventeenth-century deism, eighteenth-century rationalism, and nineteenth-century liberalism smudged this clarity within Protestantism, at least among its academics. Shut out of his world by deists, silenced by Kant's critical philosophy, and identified by Schleiermacher with what Lutheran pietists felt about him (a major scaling down), God so shrank in men's minds that the miraculous realities of regeneration and inspiration became incredible to them. The church came to be seen as either a voluntary ethical association maintained by priestcraft in some cases and by state patronage in others, or as the state itself striking moral attitudes; and the Bible was viewed as a testament of religion, a documentary record of how God was sought and found, containing more of men's spotty and uneven thoughts about God than of God's true and abiding thoughts about man. The function of Scripture, thus conceived, in relation to the church, thus conceived, was to give moral inspiration and emotional encouragement rather than to rule for God by mediating his instruction and direction. In this way the Bible, which the Reformers venerated as in Calvin's phrase "the sceptre of God," the instrument of divine government, came to be regarded as an instrument rather of human culture, and among Protestant leaders of thought the original Protestant understanding of biblical authority was almost wholly eclipsed.

In this century, the Bible-church relationship has become a major theme of discussion once more. As the turn-of-the-century optimism of religious as well as political liberals shrivelled in Europe and Britain through the impact of the First World War, and in North America a decade later through the impact of the Great Depression, Protestants began to realize afresh that the church is God's sinful, needy people living only by his word of grace, and that Scripture, which witnesses to God's word and work of mercy for his people in the past, is the trysting place where he meets and addresses his church today. The names of Barth, Brunner, and Reinhold Niebuhr call for honorable mention among exponents of this emphasis. Faith in Scripture as the record and medium of revelation revived, and faith in the living God of Scripture seemed to revive with it. "Biblical theology" appeared, announcing itself as a full-fledged exegetico-theological discipline whereby you read canonical Scripture "from within," as a corporate confession of faith in the God of redemptive history; you identify with that faith; and you thenceforth tackle all questions of truth and obedience in directly biblical terms. Roman Catholic and ecumenical theologians took up "biblical theology," and many fine expositions of the Bible "from within" have been produced during the past forty years, imparting to the church everywhere a more vivid sense of its continuity and indeed identity with the church of the Old and New Testaments than it had known for many a long day.

Among scholars, however, "biblical theology" has for more than a decade been under a cloud. Its assumption of the unity of biblical teaching is on the shelf while the hypothesis of an ultimate plurality of biblical theologies is explored, and the instability and incoherence which always marked it, but which its first practitioners had hoped to transcend, are frequently and mercilessly highlighted. Its defects unfortunately are real, and go deep. As I pointed out in 1958,[1] the "biblical theology" program as presented by its architects suffers from unending oscillations because it refuses *a priori* to identify with the uniform biblical belief in totally trustworthy Scriptures, but rests on the standard type of academic biblical criticism which treats as possibly or actually false much that the Bible presents as true. This inconsistent streak of skepticism, violating the movement's own announced method, has, as I predicted,[2] become its Achilles' heel. From its own ranks have come scholars urging that theology must face the overall historical uncertainty of Scripture; that the overlay of interpretation in biblical narrative means we regularly cannot be sure what actually happened, i.e., what we could have seen and verified had we been there; that no one "biblical way of thinking" and no unique "Hebrew mentality" (as was once rashly claimed) can be shown to exist; that since different theologies and historical approaches, brought to Scripture, yield different interpretations of key points, biblical authority is hopelessly problematical; and that there is no good reason anyway to treat the fruits of historical exegesis and criticism as theologically normative.[3] These problems of relating narrative to fact and part to part within the Bible cannot be opened up here, but it can be said at once that they look insoluble on any other basis than that the canonical Scriptures are what the biblical authors and precritical expositors took them to be, namely God's witness to himself in the form of celebratory, reflective, and didactic witness to him by men who "moved by the Holy Spirit spoke from God" (2 Pet. 1:21). On this basis, however, "biblical theology" can I think be put back on the road academically,[4] and this is certainly desirable, for when consistently pursued it is wholly right-minded. Plainly as an academic discipline it fell on its face through trying to go too far too fast and too unsteadily, without enough methodological reflection on what it was doing; equally plainly, however, it is in essence the approach of the great body of theologically significant biblical expositors from Irenaeus to Barth, just as it is the technical statement of the approach which I ventured to spell out earlier as the wayfarer's path to understanding.[5] So it needs to be rehabilitated, not abandoned.

Meantime, the new biblical interest has borne many encouraging fruits. The Council of Trent was long thought to teach that unwritten traditions and the written Scriptures were two separate sources of divine truth, but now it has been shown that this is not necessarily so,[6] and Vatican II spoke of tradition as simply the church's deepening understanding of the Scriptures.[7] More and more Roman Catholic theologians, with Karl Rahner, nowadays the dean of them,[8] are recognizing an obligation to show that each particular tradition has an adequate biblical base. Major ecumenical studies of tradition have been made,[9] with Protestants showing a new interest in tradition as the initial exposition of Scripture which the church hands on to nurture each new generation. The stress which all denominations exhibit on lay Bible study and biblical preaching in worship testifies to a widespread sense that Scripture must, and can, renew the church—a sense, be it said, no less strong among Roman Catholics than among Protestants.[10] All these developments raise again the old problem: how should the proper relationship between Bible and church be formulated in theory, and how can it be realized in practice?

Bible

It will help us in discussing these questions if we first spend a little time defining our terms.

What is *the Bible*? On the face of it, it is a library—a collection of sixty-six separate items, written in three languages (Hebrew, Aramaic, Greek), composed and brought together over a period of more than a thousand years, and containing material of the most varied literary types—written-up history, personal memoirs, sermons, letters, hymns, prayers, love poetry, philosophical poetry, family trees, visions, tales, statistics, public laws, rubrics for rituals, inventories, and much else. It divides into two collections, the second dating from a single half-century (hardly more, and perhaps much less) hundreds of years after the composing of the first collection ended. You might have expected this mass of material to be classified as a compendium of Jewish and Christian classics, or something like that.

But nothing of the kind! From the start the Christian church has treated the two collections with their varied contents as a unified whole. It was doing this at the end of the first century, before it had a single name for them, when what we call the Old Testament was "the Scriptures" and what we call the New Testament was "the Gospel and the Apostles." For all the books to appear, as now they do, in one thousand-plus-page volume called "the Holy Bible" (singular) makes explicit the view of their unity that was always implicit in the church's use of them. The Christian idea of Scripture as the God-given *canon* (measuring rod, standard, ruler, rule) came from Judaism and the Old Testament. The church, taught by the apostles, claimed the Jewish Scriptures as written by divine inspiration to instruct Christians (cf. Rom. 15:4, cf. 3:2, 16:26; 1 Cor. 9:9 f., 10:11; 1 Pet. 1:10-12); bracketed with them a selection of documents containing apostolic witness to Christ (cf. 2 Pet. 3:16); and formed at once the habit of elucidating texts and establishing tenets by cross-reference to other parts of the whole collection, just as the rabbis, Jesus and several New Testament authors had done in handling the Old Testament. This habit proclaims the assumption that the entire collection forms a unity. But many, we know, who have tried to read the Bible have got lost in it and found no way to put it all together; can the assumption of unity be justified? The answer is: yes, and at two distinct levels.

First, the sixty-six books have a demonstrable unity of subject matter and standpoint, a unity that links Genesis, Judges, Job and Jeremiah with Matthew, Acts, Romans and Revelation and all that lies between. Each book proves on inspection to be recounting or anticipating or reflecting on or giving thanks for part or all of the work of the Creator who is also the Redeemer, and who acts to set up his kingdom of grace in and over human lives. This work of God in both the space-time continuum of world history and in his personal dealings with individuals is the story line of the Bible. The story has one hero (the triune Jehovah, Father, Son, and Holy Spirit), one theme (life for sinful mankind through Jesus Christ by faith), and a unified plot. Opening with tragedy (man pitchforked into ruin: the fall and the flood), the plot moves to a long episodic buildup (the call of Abraham and the career of his descendants, two captivities, one in Egypt and one in Babylon, two exoduses, an earthly kingdom that rises and wanes, hope of an eternal kingdom that grows steadily stronger as human prospects wither). The climax comes with a catastrophic reversal of apparent disaster (the Son of God arrives and is killed; but he rises to reign, sends the Spirit, and pledges his return; through his atoning death sinners are saved, the kingdom of grace is fully revealed, and the woman's seed triumphs). The story locates our lives between Christ's two comings and directs us to trust him as our Savior, Lord, and Deliverer from the wrath to come (cf. 1 Thess. 1:10); it is thus *kerygma* (proclamation), the sum and substance of the gospel message. The story is also the reference point for books of doctrine (e.g., Romans), ethics (e.g., Proverbs; Hosea; James), and devotion (e.g., the Psalms); you cannot understand these books properly till you slot them into their place in the history, on which in fact they are all in one way or another responsive comments, interpretative, celebratory, and applicatory. Read the Bible with something other than the ongoing story as your key, and you may well feel lost and wonder how it all hangs together. But read it in terms of the story, and amazement at its inner unity is likely to overwhelm you.

It was Irenaeus, reacting against Marcion and other Gnostics when they denied the identity of the God of the Old Testament and the God of the New, who in the second century pioneered the highlighting of the Bible's unity of plot, and in our day "biblical theology," reacting against liberal denials of redemptive continuity between the two Testaments, has highlighted the point again. As a result, presentations of the Bible as *drama* (how our redemption was won) and as *witness* to the God who loves, seeks, and saves has effectively displaced the older liberal account of it as a treasury of religious experience, the viewpoint embodied in such books as E. F. Scott's *Varieties of New Testament Religion* (1943). Whereas the first half of this century saw such publications as *The Bible Designed to Be Read as Literature* (a title which G. B. Bentley described as a gravestone for the word of God[11]), popular accounts of the Bible for the post-Second World War generation had titles like *The Book of the Acts of God* (G. Ernest Wright and Reginald Fuller).[12] The change reflected a great recovery of understanding.

Nor is this all. In elucidating the unity of the Bible there is, second, the fact of inspiration to be reckoned with. Scripture is God's own teaching!—that was Paul's meaning when he wrote in 2 Timothy 3:16 that all Scripture (he meant, our Old Testament) is *theopneustos* (God-breathed, a product of the creative breath which according to Psalm 33:6 made the heavens).[13] To this conviction New Testament writers testify every time they cite an Old Testament passage as bringing Christians God's message.[14] Hereby they show their certainty that God gave these Scriptures by a special exercise of his providence in order to "instruct . . . for salvation through faith in Christ Jesus," and equip for every good work, generations unborn at the time of writing (cf. 2 Tim. 3:15-17). That the books are fully human is not nor ever was in question; the point is that they are profitable for Christians because they have ultimately a divine origin and carry a divine message for Christians, having been given by God with Christians in mind. So what Peter says of the prophets—"men they were, but, impelled by the Holy Spirit, they spoke the words of

God" (2 Pet. 1:21, NEB: "what came from God"
would be closer to the Greek than "the words of
God," though the thought as paraphrased is right)—
should be said of all Old Testament writers, whatever
the literary type of their work and however it was
composed.

It is clear that the psychological method and phenomena of divine inspiration varied from one writer
to another, and from time to time for the same writer. The inspiration of the prophet delivering (and
also recording or dictating, cf. Jer. 36) God's oracles
was psychologically *dualistic,* in the sense that he
knew himself to be relaying what he had received,
with no admixture of his own thoughts (whatever he
might have contributed to its poetic form). The inspiration of the historian was psychologically *didactic,*
in the sense that he evidently wrote on the basis of
research into facts and traditions and reflection on
the most instructive shape to give his material. Something similar should be said about the wisdom writers, and about the anonymous editors and redactors
who worked to give prophetic and historical books
their final form. The inspiration of psalmists was psychologically *responsive* and *creative,* in the sense that
they crafted into shape the praises and prayers that
welled up within them as they looked towards God,
just as do secular poets and song writers in working
up their ideas for secular lyrics. But the point to note
is that whatever the psychological mode of inspiration, the theological reality of it was the same
throughout. The books, like their authors, are fully
human, but their message is also, and equally, divine.

New Testament inspiration is of the same three
types: dualistic (Revelation), didactic (the Gospels,
Acts and Epistles) and lyric (hymns and doxologies);
each type corresponding closely to its Old Testament
counterpart.

The inspiration of Scripture, as defined, is commonly regarded today as dubious and problematical, not to say incredible, but for New Testament Christians, teachers and taught alike, it was axiomatic. Why this difference? It is not enough to say that we are aware of critical questions about the truth of the Old Testament of which New Testament Christians were not aware; had they known of them, it would not have affected their attitude. For they had a compelling positive reason for accepting Scripture as instruction direct from their God. Not only was this view of Scripture basic to the Jewish faith out of which Christianity came, it was basic also to the ministry of Jesus himself. When Jesus said, "Think not that I have come to abolish the law and the prophets; I have come not to abolish them but to fulfil them" (Mt. 5:17)—a claim which is in truth the hinge on which the whole New Testament view of Christianity turns—he explicitly took his stand under the authority of Scripture; while differing from others on its interpretation at certain key points, he endorsed completely the received view of its nature and normative force, as *torah* (authoritative instruction) from the Creator, his Father. The apostles did not fail to follow their Master here. As I wrote elsewhere,

Christ and his apostles quote Old Testament texts not merely as what, e.g., Moses, David or Isaiah said (see Mk. 7:10, 12:36, 7:6; Rom. 10:5, 11:9, 10:20, etc.), but also as what God said through these men (see Acts 4:25, 28:25, etc.), or sometimes simply what "he" (God) says (e.g., 2 Cor. 6:16; Heb. 8:5, 8), or what the Holy Ghost says (Heb. 3:7, 10:15). Furthermore, Old Testament statements, not made by God in their contexts, are quoted as utterances of God (Mt. 19:4 f.; Heb. 3:7; Acts 13:34 f.; citing Gen. 2:24; Ps. 95:7; Is. 55:2 respectively). Also, Paul refers to God's promise to Abraham and

his threat to Pharaoh, both spoken long before the biblical record of them was written, as words which *Scripture* spoke to these two men (Gal. 3:8; Rom. 9:17); which
shows how completely he equated the statements of
Scripture with the utterance of God.[15]

Clearly it was as much part of New Testament Christianity to receive as divine teaching the Old Testament, which witnessed to Christ and which he fulfilled, as it was to receive the message of Jesus and his
apostles as divine teaching.

It is indeed scarcely possible to account for the
staggering unity of standpoint and subject matter on
which I commented above without positing inspiration. Four centuries ago John Calvin appealed to the
"beautiful harmony of all its parts"[16] as confirming
belief in the Bible's divine origin and authority, and
in this as in so much else Calvin's judgment was
sound. There is no doubt that Calvin, who always
treated biblical teaching as God's instruction and
affirmed that all believers knew it to be so through
the inner witness of the Spirit, held the view of inspiration outlined above.[17] It is ironical that in our
time Reformed churches generally should have been
so overawed by the supposedly sure results of biblical
criticism (which, being loaded from the start with
skeptical assumptions, could not but come up with
skeptical conclusions) as largely to give up Calvin's
view; doubly ironical when one observes that the
most recent ecclesiastical witness to it of any standing
has been borne by the Church of Rome! The statement of Vatican II on biblical inspiration merits
quotation in full.

Those divinely revealed realities which are contained
and presented in sacred Scripture have been committed
to writing under the inspiration of the Holy Spirit. Holy

Mother Church, relying on the belief of the apostles, holds that the books of both the Old and New Testaments in their entirety, with all their parts, are sacred and canonical because, having been written under the inspiration of the Holy Spirit (cf. Jn. 20:31; 2 Tim. 3:16; 2 Pet. 1:19-21; 3:15-16) they have God for their author and have been handed on as such to the Church herself. In composing the sacred books, God chose men, and while employed by him they made use of their own powers and abilities; thus with him acting in them and through them, they, as true authors, consigned to writing everything and only those things which he wanted.

Therefore, since everything asserted by the inspired authors or sacred writers must be held to be asserted by the Holy Spirit, it follows that the books of Scripture must be acknowledged as teaching firmly, faithfully, and without error that truth which God wanted put into the sacred writings for the sake of our salvation. Therefore "all Scripture is inspired by God and useful for teaching, for reproving, for correcting, for instruction in righteousness; that the man of God may be perfect, equipped for every good work" (2 Tim. 3:16-17).

In sacred Scripture, therefore, while the truth and holiness of God always remain intact, the marvellous "condescension" of eternal wisdom is clearly shown, "that we may learn the gentle kindness of God, which words cannot express, and how far he has gone in adapting his language with thoughtful concern for our weak human nature." For the words of God, expressed in human language, have been made like human discourse, just as of old the Word of the eternal Father, when he took to himself the weak flesh of humanity, became like other men.[18]

Sadly, some Roman Catholic theologians twist the second of these paragraphs to mean "limited inerrancy"—that is, that not everything in Scripture is "truth which God wanted put into the sacred writings for the sake of our salvation," and that what does not come in that category cannot always be trusted.[19] Yet in itself, naturally understood, this is as fine a statement of what Protestants and Roman Catholics once held in common as one could wish for. It will be a happy day when Protestants again confess the truth about Scripture in terms like these, grounding its unity of subject matter in the unity of God, it primary author.

Church

Such is the Bible. What, now, do we mean when we speak of the church?

In the New Testament the church is a many-sided reality which is spoken of from various points of view. In this essay, however, the viewpoint is precise and constant. By the church I mean, not "the whole number of the elect" (to quote Westminster Confession, 25.i), nor the organized regional or denominational federations (the Church of South India, the Anglican church, the Assemblies of God or whatever), but the pilgrim people of God on earth as such. The church is that historically continuous society which traces its lineage back to the apostles and the day of Pentecost, and behind that to Abraham, father of the faithful, whose "seed" the church is through faith in and union with Abraham's primary seed, Jesus Christ (cf. Rom. 4:16; Gal. 3:7-20). It is God's adopted family of sons and heirs, bound to him as he is bound to it in the bonds of his gracious covenant. It is also the body and bride of Jesus Christ, the "company of faithful men" *(coetus fidelium)* who enjoy union and communion with the Mediator through the Holy Spirit. As Luther rightly said, the church is essentially invisible, an object of faith rather than of sight, for the realities which constitute it—the glorified Christ who is its head, and faith which embraces him, and the Spirit who unites us with him and communicates his gifts to us—are not open to observation nor detectable by any physical test at present, whatever may become the case when Christ returns. But the church becomes visible in its local assemblies, each of which is the body of Christ in manifestation, an outcrop, specimen, sample, and microcosm of the church as a whole. It becomes visible by its association, fellowship and witness, by the preaching and sharing of God's word which it sponsors, by its administering of the sacraments of entry and continuance according to Christ's command, and by its commitment to the work which the Master gave it to do.

Now it is the nature of the church to live under the authority of Jesus Christ as its teacher no less than as its king and its priest. The church depends on the Lord Jesus for instruction in spiritual things, and looks to the Spirit of Jesus to teach these things in the Savior's name. This is true of both "Catholic" and "Protestant" outlooks. The standard Roman Catholic claim is that the church (defined, of course, in terms of communion with the Pope), being the extension of the incarnation, the prolonging in space and time of Christ's presence in this world, actually partakes of the divine infallibility and teaching authority that belong to the Lord himself. These qualities, according to the theory, find definitive expression when the Pope speaking *ex cathedra*, that is, in his official character as the teacher of Christendom exercising his *magisterium*, confirms the declarations of councils or in his own person defines convictions which the Holy Spirit is held to have established in the church's corporate mind. Eastern Orthodoxy and Anglo-

122

Catholicism, while rejecting the doctrine of the papacy, appeal similarly to the authority of the church's corporate mind down the ages ("holy Tradition"). It is important to see that these appeals to the church for doctrine, which to Protestants might look like ways of manufacturing truths and facts (lineal apostolic succession, localized eucharistic presence, the papal office itself, the Immaculate Conception and Assumption of Mary, etc.) contrary to the Spirit's teaching from Scripture, are actually expressions, however mistaken, of the same concern to be taught by Jesus Christ which makes Protestants pore over the Bible. That "man shall not live by bread alone, but by every word that proceeds from the mouth of God" (Mt. 4:4, citing Deut. 8:3) is common ground; the difference is over how God teaches. There can be no disputing that churchmanship means discipleship, and discipleship means learning, and learning means listening to the word of the Lord. Well did Luther define the church—in a way, he claimed, that a child of seven could grasp!—as "those who hear the shepherd's voice" (an echo, of course, of John 10:27). Concern to hear Christ's voice and be taught by him is basic to the identity of both the Christian and the church.

The Bible Over the Church

These characterizations of the book of which the church is the people, and of the people whose book it is, pave the way to the question, what is the proper relation of church and Bible to each other? In answer to it I offer these two propositions: first, *it is for the Bible to form and reform the church;* second, *it is for the church to keep and keep to the Bible.* Let us explore them in order.

It is for the Bible to form and reform the church. This assertion breaks down into four.

First, the church's corporate life must be shaped by the gospel.

By "gospel" (literally, "the news," "the good news") I mean here the whole "word of God" which the apostles preached and taught, embodying the "word of God" which came from Jesus (cf. Lk. 5:1, 8:11, 21, 11:28; Acts 4:31, 8:14, 11:1, 13:7, 44, 46; Col. 1:25; 1 Thess. 2:13; 1 Tim. 2:9)—in other words, the whole Christian message: the facts of Jesus' life, death, rising, reign, and future return, his missionary commission, institution of the sacraments, and sending of the Spirit (for which see the Gospels and Acts), plus Old Testament facts forming the background (as recounted in, e.g., Acts 7, 13:17 ff., and interpreted in, e.g., Gal. 3-4; Rom. 4, 9-11; Hebrews), plus theological analysis, with ethical corollaries, of God's eternal plan of grace, his "whole counsel" which has Christ and the church at its heart (Acts 20:27: see the church Epistles). It is through response to this message in credence and commitment that the church comes to exist in God's presence as a company of believers, and to take form locally before men's eyes as a visibly organized fellowship. When Anglican Article Nineteen defines the visible church as "a congregation of faithful men, in the which the pure Word of God is preached, and the Sacraments be duly ministered according to Christ's ordinance in all those things that of necessity are requisite to the same," it is specifying the principle that the New Testament message must shape the faith, life, and order of God's pilgrim people at all points. It is true that Protestants have differed as to how far New Testament descriptions of church life then have prescriptive force for church life now in such matters as

liturgy, ministerial order, and synods, but what is at
issue here is interpretation, not authority. On the de-
cisiveness of biblical principles there has been agree-
ment; the debate has had to do only with what those
principles are—whether the New Testament should
be read as setting forth by precept and precedent a
universally required church order, as some Presbyterians, Baptists, and Brethren have thought, or as
leaving the church freedom (and so imposing on it
responsibility) to implement general principles about
church fellowship and ministry in the way that seems
best in our situation, just as we see New Testament
Christians doing in their situation—which is how
other Presbyterians, with Anglicans and Lutherans
and Methodists, have seen the matter. But all Protestants agree that neither their own church order nor
any other can be justified save as a direct response to
New Testament teaching. Responsive conformity to
Christ and his gospel is acknowledged by all, as was
said above, to be the very foundation and essence of
the church's identity.

*Second, our only access to the gospel is through the Scrip-
tures.*

This is first a historical point: the New Testament
books are the prime witnesses to what Christ and the
apostles taught. They are authentic and responsible
sources, contemporary or near-contemporary with
the events recorded,[20] and no other independent
sources of any significance are available.[21] But it is
also a theological point: the New Testament, as we
saw, is Spirit-inspired apostolic witness, and Christ
meant this witness to fix the church's faith for all
time. That is implied by his prayer, "I do not pray for
these only, but also for those who are to believe in me
through their word" (Jn. 17:20). Historically, as Protestant apologists urge against Rome, no one can tell if

post-apostolic traditions, allegedly apostolic in origin, really are so. Theologically, as Oscar Cullmann says, the mid-second-century recognition of apostolic writings as *canonical*—that is, as the decisive rule for faith and life—shows clear awareness that post-apostolic tradition and apostolic tradition are not on a par, but that the latter must control and correct the former. Cullmann's words are:

> By establishing the *principle* of a Canon the Church ... drew a line under the apostolic tradition. She declared implicitly that from that very moment every subsequent tradition must be submitted to the control of the apostolic tradition. In other terms, she declared: here is the tradition which *constituted* the Church, which imposed itself on her. ... To establish a Canon is equivalent to recognizing: henceforth our ecclesiastical tradition needs to be controlled; with the help of the Holy Spirit it will be controlled by the apostolic tradition fixed in writing. ... To fix a canon was to say: henceforth we renounce the right to consider as a norm other traditions that are not fixed by the Apostles in writing. ... To say that the writings brought together in a Canon should be considered as *norm* was to say that they should be considered as *sufficient*. The teaching office of the Church was not abdicated by this final act of fixing the Canon, but its future activity was made to depend on a norm that was superior.[22]

To feel the full force of Cullmann's point, we should note that the early church's concern in thus affirming the authority of apostolic tradition was evangelical and soteriological rather than ecclesiastical and juridical. In other words: the concern was not just for orthodoxy, but for the personal knowledge of salvation in Christ to which "sound words" (1 Tim. 6:3; 2 Tim. 1:13; cf. Rom. 6:17) lead on. By setting apostolic writings above all other tradition the church was consciously guarding the gospel against its perverters, and in ascribing to those writings divine authority it was both bracketing them with the Old Testament as "able to instruct you for salvation through faith in Christ Jesus" (2 Tim. 3:15) and aligning itself with the New Testament churches whose obedience to the apostolic message had actually brought them salvation. To see the canonizing process, as some seem to do, as the post-apostolic church meeting its own felt need of a court of appeal, and to consider on that basis how providence, the Spirit, study, and church authority combined to give us the books we now have, is to miss the essence of what went on. Essentially, what was happening was this: the apostolic message about redemption, which was and is part of the saving fact of Christ, was authenticating itself as from God in its written form, just as it had authenticated itself when first preached in Jerusalem, Samaria, Corinth, and Rome. Christ had authorized the apostles to declare this message with his authority, and so by the Spirit they did, both orally and in writing, and the church's historic recognition of written apostolic witness as the New Testament canon means essentially that the church acknowledges it to be God's word of salvation. Enquiry into the pedigree, use and contents of particular books can make it seem reasonable to accept them as authentic and unreasonable not to, but ultimately the church's acceptance of them in each generation is because they impose themselves—because, that is, the church hears in them the saving word of God.

Ridderbos focuses this by distinguishing between the canon viewed qualitatively (as the authentic, authoritative presentation of Christ) and quantitatively (as a fixed collection of books).[23] The "quantitative" question, which books should be in the collection, has prompted debate, on and off, since the second century; but the "qualitative" question, whether written apostolic witness to Christ and salvation should be a norm for all Christians, was never disputed till modern times (when all first principles, it seems, are disputed by someone or other!). No felt uncertainties or scholars' disputes about the extent of the canon, therefore, should be thought to invalidate the principle that the church's knowledge of the gospel comes ultimately through the Scriptures alone.[24]

In saying this, I do not suggest for one moment that traditions of teaching, worship, and order in the church are unimportant. On the contrary, they should be gratefully received and respectfully handled, for they are the fruit of much past effort to think and live biblically, and much of their content is plainly the result of the Spirit's teaching and application of Scripture (the ecumenical creeds, for instance, and a great deal of the local confessions, liturgies, hymns, and theological and devotional writing that particular parts of the church have produced). To say that "tradition represents the worldliness of the Church"[25] is one-sided; tradition is not always worldly and wrong. Yet the statement has a point: tradition is not always godly and right either. This is what you would expect where the Spirit is really at work among sinners who are not yet perfectly sanctified in either head or heart. And this is why all traditions must be submitted to the corrective judgment of the Scriptures which they seek to expound and apply and subserve: why, in particular, post-apostolic traditions must be brought under the control of apostolic tradition in the New Testament. As Paul in Christ's name challenged the Jerusalem church tradition which called for the circumcision of Gentile converts in Galatia, and the "human tradition" which was corrupting the doctrine, worship, and service of God through Christ at Colossae (Col. 2:8); as also our Lord in his Father's name challenged the rabbinic expository tradition as corrupting and evading the divine law (cf. Mk. 7:5-13; Mt. 5:20-48); so Paul and his fellow witnesses who wrote the New Testament, and Christ himself speaking in and through them, must be allowed to challenge our own latter-day traditions. Only that which is demonstrably rooted in Scripture, and which therefore we can be sure the apostles would have endorsed, can be held to belong to the gospel, or to be needed for personal spiritual health or the church's corporate pleasing of God.

Third, the Scriptures interpret themselves clearly to the people of God through the Holy Spirit.

It is sad to find a Protestant author declaring that "as the Roman Church has clearly and consistently taught, the Bible needs an interpreter; it does not bear its plain meaning on its face."[26] The statement is not even half true. The testimony both of Protestant history over four and a half centuries and also of the ecumenical biblical movement till very recently[27] is that those who will read the Bible "from within," letting it speak for itself in its own terms, reach remarkable unanimity as to its meaning.[28] Nor should this surprise us, for the inspired books were written not to mystify but to be understood, and the Spirit who gave them is with the church to interpret them, by enabling us to grasp their message in its application to ourselves. The Reformers spoke in this connection of the *clarity* or *perspicuity* of Scripture. They were not denying that Scripture sometimes alludes to things of which we have insufficient knowledge fully to explain the reference (e.g., baptism for the dead at Corinth, 1 Cor. 15:29; Christ preaching to the antediluvian spirits in prison, 1 Pet. 3:19; the "man of sin" in 1 Thess.

2:3-5; etc.); nor were they denying that secondary and incidental matters in Scripture are sometimes less than clear. Their point was that the main things, the things that the writers themselves were concerned to stress, are so fully and plainly presented that none who bring to the Bible an honest willingness to meet and know God, and to be changed by him, will miss them. The discovery that on the essentials Scripture can speak for itself was one mainspring of the Reformation, and has animated evangelical religion ever since. To allege at this stage of history that the Bible "does not bear its plain meaning on its face" is rather like complaining that television sets do not work. Millions can testify that they work very well if you know how to switch them on.

Fourth, the church, once formed, needs constantly to be reformed by the Bible.

We have already reminded ourselves that the believers who make the church are a community of imperfectly sanctified sinners; now we should link with that the New Testament vision of the church as under constant attack from "principalities . . . powers . . . world rulers of this present darkness . . . spiritual hosts of wickedness in the heavenly places" (Eph. 6:12), and face the certainty that the church in this and every age will have cause to acknowledge that it has slipped and failed. Lapses into misbelief and unbelief, ethical error and compromise, apathy and superstition, formality and dead routine, must be expected, and reformation—not only in the negative sense of purging abuses (for man cannot live on disinfectant alone), but in the positive sense of *re*forming through the giving of new scriptural substance to faith and life—will be our chronic need. The old slogan, *ecclesia reformata semper reformanda* (the reformed church always needs to be reformed)

9

bears true witness to this. Today's "in words" for what I have called "reformation" are "renewal" and (in some quarters) "revival," and "reformation" is widely thought of as a less vital process, having to do with externals only; but "reformation" on sixteenth- and seventeenth-century lips meant all that these words mean and more, and I shall stay with it in making my present point.

Can Scripture reform and revitalize moribund churches—which means, the moribund individuals who make them up—in these days? It may be a sufficient answer to point out that by the Spirit's power Scripture has certainly done this in the past. Think, for instance, of some of the movements sparked off by the Spirit's application—first to individuals, then through them to communities—of just one book, filling between fifteen and twenty pages in most Bibles, Paul's letter to the Romans, which Calvin described as "a sure road . . . to the understanding of the whole Scripture." Augustine, troubled but uncommitted, read in a friend's Bible Romans 13:13 f.: "Put on the Lord Jesus Christ, and make no provision for the flesh. . . ." "A clear light flooded my heart, and all the darkness of doubt vanished away," he tells us.[29] A thoroughgoing Christian from then on, he became the foremost champion of God's free grace and the most influential teacher bar none in Western Christian history to date. Then, eleven centuries later, Martin Luther, a monk and academic theologian, but a man without peace, who had found Romans baffling because he took "the righteousness of God" (Rom. 1:17, etc.) to be God's retributive righteousness judging sin, came to see that this phrase really means "that righteousness whereby, through grace and sheer mercy, he justifies us by faith"—and at once "I felt myself to be reborn and to have gone through open doors into paradise. . . ."[30] From this discovery came the teaching that triggered all the Reformation. Two centuries after that, John Wesley, a failed missionary, heard Luther's Preface to Romans read at a meeting in London and "I felt my heart strangely warmed. I felt I did trust in Christ, Christ alone, for my salvation; and an assurance was given me that he had taken *my* sins away, even *mine;* and saved me from the law of sin and death."[31] From this experience of assurance sprang the momentous ministry which produced world Methodism. Again, in 1816 Robert Haldane expounded Romans to students in Geneva, and revival (reformation!) came to the Reformed churches of Switzerland and France; and in 1918 Karl Barth published an exposition of Romans that changed the course of twentieth-century theology. "There is no telling what may happen," wrote F. F. Bruce, "when people begin to study the Epistle to the Romans."[32] Nor is there any reason to think that the power of Romans, with the other Scriptures, to reform and revitalize Christians and churches is any less today than it was—which means that a challenge confronts us here and now to seek in order that we too may find. When you have finished reading this book, what is the next thing you will set yourself to do?

This leads to my second proposition. As it is for the Bible to form and reform the church, so *it is for the church to keep and keep to the Bible*. Consider the two points involved.

The Church Under the Bible

First, the church must keep the Bible.

This is a Reformation point. As we saw, the Bible is our only sure link with apostolic Christianity, and the only sure means whereby God's word comes to us today. It is the handiwork, gift, and textbook of the Holy Spirit, and the instrument of our Lord's royal authority. Just as the Jews were entrusted with "the oracles of God" in Old Testament times (Rom. 3:2), so the Christian church is called to be, in the words of Anglican Article Twenty, "a keeper of Holy Writ." We have already noted that God, not the church, created the canon of Scripture; he inspired the books and moved the church to receive them for what they are. The church no more created the canon than Newton created the law of gravity; recognition is not creation. Barth's dictum, "The Bible constitutes itself the canon. It is the canon because it has imposed itself upon the church, and invariably does so," has been criticized as an over-simplification,[33] but it has the same sort of clarifying thrust as does the definition of engine-drivers (North Americans would say, engineers) as a class of men whose task it is to stop trains in scheduled places at scheduled times. The church must see itself, therefore, as neither author nor lord of Scripture, but as steward of it, serving God both by observing in its own life his written requirements and also by spreading Bible truth as widely as possible so that all may learn "the message of this salvation" (Acts 13:26).

So Holy Writ is to be kept not under a bushel, but under men's noses. Its message is to be held forth as diligently as it is held fast. Churches must use all means to promote individual and corporate attention to the Bible; to recover the Bible-proclaiming, Bible-teaching ethos which was one secret of all the strength they ever had; to foster group and family Bible study; to sponsor good clear translations and expositions; and to bring the Bible to bear on theoretical problems and practical decisions alike. The church serves its Master best by keeping the Bible, not in store on the shelf as a relic of the past, but in use in each congregation as the ever-relevant handbook of authentic discipleship, received in effect from the Master himself as his means of fulfilling the divine promise and purpose of "teaching . . . reproof . . . correction and . . . training in righteousness." So any congregation in which Bibles are not in worshippers' hands at services, nor is Bible teaching the focus of attention in sermons, nor is Bible study a main activity, has cause to be ashamed of the poor quality of its discipleship.

Second, the church must keep to the Bible.

"But be doers of the word, not hearers only, deceiving your own selves," wrote James. "For if anyone is a hearer of the word and not a doer, he is like a man who observes his natural face in a mirror . . . he . . . goes away and at once forgets what he was like." Only doers are blessed (Jas. 1:22-25). "Doing the word," then—"doing the truth," "keeping his word," "keeping his commandments," in John's phrases (1 Jn. 1:6, 2:3, 5)—is the church's calling. Nothing less—no amount of idle and empty talk, however orthodox—will please God or bring us good. There must be obedience.

Here, however, a painful problem emerges. To "do the word" we must first understand it, and on biblical interpretation today the church is agonizingly divided. Hence what some see as "doing the word" in fields of sexual, medical, industrial, and political ethics is to others blatant and destructive disobedience to the word, just as what some today regard as biblical faith strikes others as antibiblical unbelief. The bewildering theological confusion, the anarchic intellectual individualism, that plagues the modern church, both Protestant and Catholic, springs directly from disagreement about the way to interpret

Scripture—that is, about the way to get at, not just its historical meaning, but what it means *for us*. Why this chaos of claims and counterclaims? asks the bemused observer. What goes on? In a nutshell, the answer is as follows.

As long as the belief in inspiration spelled out earlier in this essay was the basis of interpretative endeavor, only three divergences of principle and method were found among biblical expositors.

1. Fathers and mediaevals thought that God's message to each generation in and through the words of Scripture was sometimes, if not indeed always, cast into a code of allegorical equivalents, which it was now their task to crack; but the Reformers and their followers insisted that God's message was always found in some application of the natural meaning which the human writer's first readers would have gleaned from his words.

2. Roman Catholics held that we may read into Scripture from tradition meanings which the biblical words are capable of bearing in themselves (in relation, for instance, to the papacy or the eucharist); but Protestants maintained that we must always confine ourselves to reading out of Scripture the meaning which the words demonstrably do bear in their context.

3. Some Presbyterians, Puritans, and Brethren thought that all New Testament references to acceptable action taken in the apostolic churches have the force of command to later churches to do the same as part of their own church order; but other Protestants have not thought so.

All particular differences of understanding used to be located within the parameters which these three divergences set. But since biblical criticism got into its stride and Protestants started reading Scripture as relaying men's thoughts rather than God's teaching, the possibilities of interpretative difference have greatly multiplied and the task of discerning what each such difference implies has become far harder. In terms of approach and method there are nowadays, broadly speaking, three main types of interpreters.

1. There are those, Protestant and Catholic, who uphold the church's historic belief in biblical inspiration. Beyond that, they divide among themselves along the old lines. These conservatives mean by interpretation applying to ourselves the doctrinal and moral instruction of the Bible, read as an historically structured, self-authenticating and self-interpreting organism of revealed truth. Patristic expositor-theologians like Chrysostom and Augustine, and Protestant expositor-theologians like Calvin, Owen, Matthew Henry, Charles Hodge, William Hendriksen, and the great if strange Karl Barth, have gone this way. It is essentially the approach which Childs calls "canonical," and defends as such. (Childs, like Barth, declines to ground the instrumentality of Scripture in mediating God's word to his people on an inspiration which entails the inerrancy of Scripture as given; but Barth, at least, invariably treated Scripture as inerrant in every aspect of its witness to God's facts and their meanings, and he who does this cleaves in practice to the method we are describing here, even if his theoretical account of it falls short and his theology raises other problems.)

2. There are those, Protestant and Catholic, who view Scripture as witness to God by godly men who, though they thought wrongly of him at some points, thought rightly and profoundly of him at others. The fallibility of the witnesses, which some highlight and others play down, is universally

allowed for, and arguments are constantly being mounted from the coherence of this or that assertion with the main stream of biblical thought to justify accepting the assertion as true. The (curious?) basis of the reasoning is that the Bible as a whole can't be wrong, though individual contributors to it can. However, tracing out the historical growth and coherence of biblical testimony is an important exercise in its own right, and it is all gain that expositors of this school work so hard at it, however little the skepticism that sets them going may seem justifiable. These moderns mean by interpretation distinguishing true views of God and life from the rest of what is in the Bible—isolating its core, essence, overall thrust or central witness, as they would say—and applying to us what they have selected. Their canon of truth and wisdom is thus narrower than the canon of Scripture, and their decisions as to which biblical assertions to discard and which biblical absolutes to relativize are bound to seem arbitrary both to colleagues who operating on the same principle make different decisions, and to those who allow weight to the claim that (not some but) all Scripture is God-breathed. The approach I am describing is essentially that of the temporarily derailed "biblical theology" movement, of which Childs wrote: "One of the major factors in the breakdown . . . was its total failure to come to grips with the inspiration of Scripture. The strain of using orthodox Biblical language for the constructive part of theology, but at the same time approaching the Bible with all the assumptions of liberalism, proved in the end to cause an impossible tension."[34] Sadly, the large ecumenical community of scholars who still follow this method seem not to see the intrinsic oddity of what they are doing when they pick and choose within the Bible; it is of course always hard to discern oddity in an accepted communal activity.

3. There are those, mainly though not invariably Protestant, for whom the New Testament (the Old is a separate problem) is a culturally determined verbalization of ineffable existential encounters with God. These interpreters make two assumptions. The first is that God does not communicate with men through language. The second is that biblical thoughts about relations with him are "mythological" constructs in the sense that they function not as windows through which we watch God at work and so learn his ways, but as mirrors in which we see reflected the minds of the men whose encounters with God the myths objectify. What we learn from this is precisely their "self-understanding"—which, indeed, we may then come to share as our living though voiceless Creator similarly encounters us. This is the theme of Bultmannian hermeneutics, on which busy scholars have rung many changes in our time. The exponents of this "new hermeneutic" as it is called see interpretation as the task of so explicating the biblical verbal matrix by historical exegesis and so manipulating it in sermons as to promote in folk at the receiving end the same sort of subjective events that first produced it. They insist that one can only witness to encounter with God by mythology, which expresses and may spark off a new self-understanding, but which tells nothing about God save that he produced the self-understanding.

My line of argument in this book implies that the church can only in principle keep to the Bible as it interprets Scripture by method (1). Methods (2) and (3) embody grains of truth which exponents of method (1) must never forget—that Scripture is no less human for being inspired, for instance, and that its verbal form is culturally conditioned every-where—but as alternatives to method (1) they fail. Those who espouse them do so in good faith subjectively, but that does not alter the fact that they cannot yield good faith objectively. Where they dominate, truth and power fail, churchmen live in the dark spiritually, neither the triune God nor the gospel nor God's moral will are clearly known, and deadening and destructive confusion reigns, both in beliefs and in morals. We see this around us today. Both faithfulness and fruitfulness depend on adhering to method (1).

This is a sad conclusion, for much of the church today is effectively committed to these more or less mistaken methods, and a great part of the academic theological community lines up to stop people embracing method (1) as God-wrought spiritual instinct would lead them to do, lest they lapse into some form of obscurantism. To be sure, there has been obscurantism among simple adherents of method (1), just as there has been among sophisticated exponents of methods (2) and (3); but to blackball method (1) on this account is like forbidding us to go out and walk in the sunshine for fear that while doing so we might fall and break a leg, as someone or other once did. The truth is that if the church is ever again going to live happily and fruitfully with the Bible—which means, happily and fruitfully with its Lord, who rules by means of the Bible—it must stop retreating from the ghost of an untheological inerrancy, and once more embrace the whole Bible as the written word of God and interpret it on the basis that it neither misinforms nor misleads.

When Harold Lindsell puts the finger on teaching institutions in USA which have recently given up their corporate commitment to method (1), he touches only the tip of the iceberg. Most centers where the church's future salaried instructors are trained gave up any such commitment long ago. Lindsell was right to focus on seminaries; what they are today the whole church is likely to be tomorrow. Seminaries and theological colleges are strategic places. The church will not learn to handle Scripture aright while budding clergy are taught to handle it wrongly.

Only by the grace of God through the Bible does the church ever learn to keep to the Bible. It is plain that the church needs much of that grace today. Whether Scripture will effectively reestablish its authority over the modern church remains to be seen. Vindicating the principle of "canonical" inerrancy, that is, an inerrancy shaped by exegesis and theology rather than by secular preoccupations, is a beginning, but no more.[35] The vagaries of current critical and hermeneutical opinion are desperately daunting, yet it is clear that desire to hear the word of God from Scripture burns strong in Christian minds all round the world, and this is a hopeful sign. Perhaps the present pages may do something under God to deepen and direct that desire. Certainly, they could fulfill no higher ministry in the church at this time.

Three Reviews

Holy Scripture, by G. C. Berkouwer. Grand Rapids: Eerdmans, 1975. 377 pp., $8.95.

Berkouwer, the learned, warm-hearted and irenical professor (now emeritus) of systematic theology in the Free University, Amsterdam, has been writing his *Studies in Dogmatics* since 1947, and this is the fifteenth of the series to appear in English. It condenses, by about a third, two Dutch volumes dating from 1966 and 1967. The translator explains the slimming process as designed to make the book "more understandable to the non-specialist."

Oh dear. I don't read Dutch and can't check the extent or effect of this bowdlerizing, but on general grounds I wish it hadn't been tried. Translators are not impresarios, and for a translator to abridge at his own discretion is unfair to any author. (I note the absence of any statement suggesting that Berkouwer approves of what has been done.)

Also, abridgment is unfair to the readers, who are left wondering what has been kept from them, and what skeletons might be in the cupboard! Earlier volumes in this notable series were translated intact, and this one should have been too. Even now it is dense reading, and I cannot see many non-specialists getting through it.

Berkouwer, as always, has three aims: to let Scripture itself speak; to restate the theology of the Reformers and those latter-day Reformed giants, Kuyper and Bavinck; and to interact with queries about the Reformed tradition, and alternatives to it, which history has thrown up. Here his thesis is that in confessing Scripture to be the Word of God its character as *human* witness to Christ must be thought through more thoroughly than conservative Protestantism and Roman Catholicism have tended to do in the past.

His own attempt to do this in relation to all the major themes in the doctrine of Scripture is so learned and wise as to make his book a milestone among conservative statements. Perhaps the best pages are those on the witness of the Spirit and the canon, but it is all good.

One feature, however, disfigures. Berkouwer's strength lies in his clear awareness that Christian conviction about the "God-breathedness" of Scripture is a matter of faith rather than of rational proof, and is inseparable from faith in the Christ to whom Scripture points. So far, so good; but this very strength brings weakness.

The weakness appears when Berkouwer berates American fundamentalists and others for their "docetic" concept of Scripture (not taking its humanness seriously, he says), and their stress on formal biblical inerrancy, a concept which he finds needless and unhelpful. These polemics show limitations in Berkouwer's own thinking.

What some, at least, of those accused of docetism are actually doing is emphasizing that Scripture must be understood, in the last analysis, as *divine* witness to Christ given in and through the human witness. This is a theme which Berkouwer does not develop. And the point being made when inerrancy is asserted is that biblical teaching, factual as well as doctrinal, is *all truth:* which is (though Berkouwer seems not to see it) an important thing to say.

Berkouwer's writings reveal no interest in the task of exhibiting faith as reasonable; nor does he display concern at the confusion that has come into theology through arbitrary rejection of things that Scripture teaches. Here, it seems, are the roots of his lack of interest in inerrancy as the true bulwark against picking and choosing within the Bible.

These are his oversights rather than his insights. For the kind of theology that he himself does so well cannot be justified to a skeptical church and an unbelieving world without invoking the presupposition of biblical inerrancy.

Apart from this weakness, however, *Holy Scripture* is a fine book.

The Bible in the Balance, by Harold Lindsell. Grand Rapids: Zondervan, 1979. 384 pp., $9.95.

This is a sequel to *The Battle for the Bible* (1976), in which Lindsell argued thus:

1. Biblical inerrancy is a *truth;* inspiration entails it. Scripture is God's own witness to himself and word to us, given in the form and by the means of human authors witnessing to him and relaying instruction in his name. To this fact of inspiration the authoritative architects of biblical religion (prophets, poets, Jesus Christ, the apostles) bore full and clear testimony. So inerrancy is as much part of the "faith once for all delivered to the saints" as is Christ's teaching on re-

pentance, resurrection or marriage.

2. Biblical inerrancy is a *heritage;* historically, the Orthodox, Roman Catholic and virtually all Protestant churches have held it, and now bequeath it to us. Only in the past two centuries have any recognized theologians wobbled on it; only very recently has such wobbling become widespread.

3. Biblical inerrancy is a *watershed;* give it up, by accepting an unbiblically low view of inspiration, and downhill you go. Once let go the truth of what Scripture says about anything, even apparent trivia of nature and history, and sooner or later major items of faith will be abandoned too, so that the entire outline of supernatural faith gets fuzzed and shrunk.

4. Biblical inerrancy is a *touchstone;* by checking whether a group holds to inerrancy one can tell what hope it has of an evangelically healthy and stable future.

5. Biblical inerrancy is a *rallying point;* true evangelicals should now regroup under this flag. Lapses from inerrancy are rife among them, and these defections must now be exposed, however many faces are reddened in the process, or we are all lost.

Book two buttresses these arguments, answers their critics, and updates and supplements the sad stories which book one told. So we learn that the National Association of Evangelicals is over a barrel; the Christian Reformed and Evangelical Covenant Churches, with the Assemblies of God and the Church of the Nazarene, are in deep trouble; the Southern Baptist Convention has gone bad, and Fuller Seminary has got worse; while for Young Life "the writing is on the wall" (p. 92). Trusted theologians (named) are slipping. Worms are in many buds. "Evangelical" is so devalued a word that we had better go back to calling ourselves fundamentalists. The domino doctrine that one thing falling brings down everything shapes all the reasoning, and the future foreseen is bleak indeed.

Opinions as to the value of book two will depend on one's estimate of the theses of book one. Let us review them.

1. Is inerrancy a revealed truth belonging to the catholic Christian heritage? YES—*but* ... the questions of inerrancy and of interpretation *must* be kept separate. Acknowledging that whatever biblical writers communicate on any subject is God-given truth does not commit you in advance to any one method or school of interpretation, nor to any one way of relating Scripture to science, nor to any one set of proposed harmonizations of inconsistent-looking texts. All it commits you to is a purpose of taking as from God all that Scripture, rightly interpreted (as you judge), proves to say. Mediaevals allegorized, Reformers interpreted literally, but both maintained inerrancy. Covenant theologians and dispensationalists, Calvinists and evangelical Arminians have significantly different hermeneutics (it's true, and we may as well admit it), but all may agree on inerrancy—as indeed they did at the Chicago conference of the International Council on Biblical Inerrancy in October 1978. Some find in Scripture wonderful anticipations of modern mathematics, physics, geology, medicine and all kinds of technology, while others on grounds of philosophy, method and technique deny that "science" in our sense appears in Scripture at all; Lindsell thinks Peter denied Christ six times, and John Wenham thinks the problem here is textual (*New Testament Studies*, July 1979, pp. 523-25); but all can join hands in affirming inerrancy, for these are differences about interpreta-

tion only. But Lindsell almost (not quite) implies that you don't believe in inerrancy unless you interpret all Scriptures as he does, and that seems to me an expository weakness.

One wishes he had somewhere highlighted that in all the communications which made up the history of revelation God accommodated himself to the historical and cultural situation of the human speaker and hearers—a situation which he, of course, had himself shaped up in readiness for each revelatory event. This does not mean that what God said was culture-bound in the sense of not applying universally, but that in applying it cultural and historical differences must be borne in mind, and no interpretation unrelated to what was being conveyed to the first addressees can be right. To say this would guide interpretation, and guard against blind reaction. For, reacting against affirmations of inerrancy that overlook accommodation, some have recently taken the position that affirming accommodation means denying inerrancy. Thus confusion is worse confounded.

2. Is inerrancy really a touchstone, watershed and rallying point for evangelicals, and did Lindsell do well to raise his voice about it? YES—*but* ... his argument in both books would gain much by re-angling. For (a) what is centrally and basically at stake in this debate, and has been ever since it began two centuries ago, is the functioning of Scripture as our authority, the medium of God's authority, for faith and life. Inerrancy is basic to authority, inasmuch as what is not true cannot claim authority in any respectable sense. But it is a further expository weakness that Lindsell nowhere focuses on biblical authority as that for the sake of which he fights the inerrancy battle. For (b) lacking this reference-point, he makes himself appear as an evangelical (or should I

say, fundamentalist) scholastic, doing theology as it were by numbers, concerned only to maintain the frozen finality of some traditional formulations of the doctrine of the nature of Scripture—and that is to make this whole discussion seem a great deal less important than it really is. Indeed, some evangelical wiseacres have written it off as trivial already; but that is not really a very discerning response.

Thank you, Harold Lindsell, for having the guts to do what you have done. To have the inerrancy question out in the open, where your writing has set it, is clarifying and catalytic. But now it really is important that we inerrantists move on to crystallize an *a posteriori* hermeneutic which does full justice to the character and content of the infallible written word *as communication*, life-embracing and divinely authoritative. Otherwise we could win "the battle for the Bible" and still lose the greater battle for the knowledge of Christ and of God in our churches, and in men's hearts.

The Authority and Interpretation of the Bible: an Historical Approach, by Jack B. Rogers and Donald K. McKim. San Francisco: Harper & Row, 1979. xxiv + 484 pp., $20.

This large-scale, well-arranged survey of some highlights in the history of Christian thought about the Bible focuses in turn on Fathers (Clement, Origen, Chrysostom, Augustine), mediaevals (Anselm, Aquinas), Reformers (Luther, Calvin), early Reformed scholastics (Peter Martyr, Zanchi, Beza), a late Reformed scholastic (Turretin), old Princetonians (Alexander, the Hodges, Warfield, Machen), anti- and non-Princetonians (Briggs, Lindsay, Orr, Forsyth, Kuyper, Bavinck), and "Recent Efforts to

Recover the Reformed Tradition" (Barth, Berkouwer, UPUSA's Confession of '67). Its main interest
is in the set of biblical questions agitated within U.S.
Presbyterianism during the past century, and this so
narrows its range as to render it, for all its length, a
monograph rather than a treatise. Its title promises
more than is performed, for interpretation (which
was not central in the Presbyterian debates) is only
touched on in its formal aspects: this leaves many
questions unanswered and some begged. (Why, for
instance, do the authors constantly oppose valuing
Scripture as a guide to Christ to valuing it as a source
of factual truth, as if historically those who valued it
as the latter lost interest in it as the former?) The
purpose of the book is stated in the preface. "We
[Presbyterians, and evangelicals generally] need a
new model, perspective or paradigm by which to view
the Bible. We believe that such a model is available in
the central Christian tradition, especially as it came to
expression at the time of the Reformation" (p. xi).
The authors' avowed aim is to review that tradition
and let it speak for itself.

There is unevenness: the sections on, for instance,
the Westminster Confession chapter 1, Barth, and
Berkouwer, are more probing and discerning than
those on, for instance, Zanchi and Turretin, whom
the authors seem to know only at second-hand.
There are slips: it was not, for instance, because Augustine saw faith as a gateway to understanding that
he was called *doctor gratiae*, the (not "a") teacher of
grace (p. 34), nor were English Puritan sermons
"often" up to four hours long (p. 211), nor was Beza a
hyper-Calvinist in the accepted sense (p. 164), nor
was the Elizabethan Church of England anything but
a Reformed church with a Reformed confession (pp.
200, 117-25). Sometimes knowledge fails: the authors

seem not to know, for instance, that "what Scripture says, God says," a phrase they seem not to like in Hodge and Warfield (p. 315, n.90), comes from Augustine, whom they applaud, or that Archibald Alexander's view of inspiration was lifted from Doddridge, whose formula Carson and Haldane laid to rest in the 1830's (pp. 272 and 321, n.235). But overall the book is well researched, clearly set out and excellently documented, and students of historical theology will find it a valuable resource.

Axe-grinding, however, cramps some parts of it. Haunted by race-memories of the fundamentalist-modernist battles of the traumatic twenties and the splits that followed, and haunted too by personal memories of having to outgrow the bold naive rationalism, as they now see it, of their own evangelical upbringing (cf. p. xi), the authors have cast the old Princeton doctrine of Holy Scripture as the villain of their piece, and composed it as, in effect, a rite of exorcism. So did James Barr write *Fundamentalism*, and both books show the same weakness—unreflective judgmentalism, reacting against what the authors now feel hurt them. Children who feel burnt dread the fire, and if they write about it ("*naughty* fire") scholarly quality is inevitably at risk.

To Rogers and McKim, the focal point of the Princeton *infame* is "the defensive, intransigent position of inerrancy . . . this scholasticizing, philosophizing phenomenon" as Ford Battles with a fine flush of adjectives calls it in his Foreword (pp. xv f.). This, apparently, they take to involve:

1. not recognizing what they call accommodation (better, condescension), whereby God in history spoke his messages within the particularity and limitations of his messengers' cultural milieu;

2. assuming therefore that God's words in

Scripture mesh in directly with the cultural milieu of its latter-day expositors (which assumption compels unhistorical exegesis);

3. in exegesis, seeking only propositional statements and their logical links and ignoring all other forms and levels of communication in Scripture;

4. disregarding Scripture's instrumental function in making Christ and salvation known to us, and concentrating instead on its perfection as a source of factual knowledge about his work;

5. reserving the right to posit textual corruption if seemingly discrepant details of our text cannot be harmonized in any other way.

However, the idea of inerrancy necessitates none of these stances, any more than it necessitates John Owen's belief that Old Testament vowel points were inspired, or Charles Hodge's over-simple view of scientific method, or Voetius's idea that Psalm 19 taught science, and a careful check of Princetonian exposition—that of J. A. Alexander, Warfield himself and Geerhardus Vos, for example—will show it to be innocent of such gaffes. The authors' contrary insinuations are a bad lapse.

I perceive that they want to see Reformed theology renewed in a form free from obscurantist naivety and backward-looking scholasticism. Good; so do I. The rational triumphalism and perfectionist tone of the old Princeton theological style smells provincial to them. Well, I cannot wonder. They see that on the relation of faith to reason, and on the matter of exegetical and theological method, the Dutchmen Kuyper, Bavinck and Berkouwer are closer at points to Calvin than were the Princetonians. Agreed, though the authors follow the crowd of Calvin expositors since Barth and imply that the gap between Calvin and old Princeton was vast, whereas study shows that in his Christian rationalism, giving reasons for faith and hacking away at the unreasonableness of infidelity, Calvin was closer to the Princetonians than to the Dutchmen. Rogers and McKim, who on the present showing are fideistic children of our anti-rational age, miss that fact, but fact it is. However, I have no basic problem with their viewpoint so far.

But when they imply that Warfield was naive to think that "all minds are after all of the same essential structure" (p. 371, n.40), and assume that the laws of logic do not apply when folk think in pictures (p. 284), and treat the Aristotelian-Thomist-Reidian epistemology as if it might have misrepresented the mental operations it describes, I begin to wonder if they know what they are talking about. And I really am startled when first they invite me by their expository style to admire Calvin against Warfield and then tell me that the cleavage was due to Calvin having "Neoplatonic presuppositions" where Warfield had "Aristotelian assumptions" (p. 334, etc.). I do not mind Rogers and McKim being Neoplatonists if they want to be, but I object to being told that I must also be one if I am to commend myself to them as a good Reformed theologian. (Is Neoplatonism a revealed truth?)

In fact, of course, when it comes to substantive assertions the only decisive question is, what is scriptural?—and this, as Calvin and Warfield knew, can only be settled by exegesis and synthetic theologizing. Nothing is resolved by using "goodie"-language of one man and "baddie"-language of another. And it is, to say the least, unhelpful so to dwell on philosophical and methodological differences between men as to cloud the fact that in their view and use of the Bible, and their understanding of the message of the gospel, they were substantially at one.

Now I saw in my dream, that when Rogers and McKim got to heaven they found two shining ones waiting arm in arm, with something to say to them. The name of the one was Calvin, and the name of the other was Warfield. I saw that the new arrivals were freely and heartily forgiven; and I was glad. So I awoke, and behold it was a dream.

Notes

Chapter 2

[1]See J. I. Packer, "Calvin's View of Scripture," in ed. J. W Montgomery, *God's Inerrant Word,* Minneapolis: Bethany Fellowship, 1974, pp. 103 f.; H. J. Forstman, *Word and Spirit: Calvin's Doctrine of Biblical Authority,* Stanford: Stanford University Press, 1962, pp. 49-62. I use "literalistic" for any way of speaking or interpreting which excludes imagery, analogy and metaphor.

[2]See the passages quoted in *God's Inerrant Word,* p. 102 f.

[3]See J. W. Montgomery, "Lessons from Luther on the Inerrancy of Holy Writ," in *op. cit.,* pp. 67 ff., with passages quoted and literature cited.

[4]See B. B. Warfield, *The Inspiration and Authority of the Bible,* Philadelphia: Presbyterian and Reformed Publishing Co., 1948; J. W. Wenham, *Christ and the Bible,* London: Tyndale Press, 1972; Louis Berkhof, *Systematic Theology: Introduction Volume,* Grand Rapids: Eerdmans, 1938.

[5]See Montgomery, *op. cit.,* pp. 78-83; M. Reu, *Luther and the Scriptures,* Columbus, Ohio: Wartburg Press, 1944, chapter III. Luther was convinced that James taught justification before God on the ground of a Christian's own works, and that one criterion of canonicity for New Testament books was apostolicity of doctrine, and that here James was contradicting the apostolic doctrine of Paul and the rest of the New Testament, preaching the law instead of the gospel.

[6]The Gallican and Belgic Confessions and the Anglican Thirty-nine Articles list the sixty-six books of the Protestant canon, as the Westminster Confession was later to do. Remarks by Reformers showing their awareness that the attestation and consequent authority of some canonical books was relatively less than

that of others were made on the basis of their own full acceptance of the canon as a whole as divinely authoritative. Apart
from Luther on James, they never dreamed of challenging the
church's historic corporate acceptance of any book on the basis
of their own present, and thus provisional, personal opinion
about it. For confessional Lutherans the extent of the canon
remains a theoretically open question, but they do not hesitate in
practice to accept the canon as we have it. The sixth of the Anglican Thirty-nine Articles identifies the canonical books as those
"of whose authority was never any doubt in the Church": this
means in the Church corporately, not in the minds of single
individuals or groups.

[7] For Calvin the analogy of faith, "to which Paul requires all
interpretation of Scripture to conform (Rom. 12:3, 6)" (*Inst.*
IV.xvii.32), relates to both the substance and the practical thrust
of doctrine (for the latter, cf. Calvin's prefatory address to the
King of France, *Institutes of the Christian Religion*, tr. F. L. Battles,
Philadelphia: Westminster Press, 1960, I.12 f.).

[8] Battles, *loc. cit.*, note 5, quotes Bucanus' 1605 definition of
the analogy of faith (clearly, to him, "the" faith, i.e., faith viewed
primarily as belief) as consisting of "the constant and perpetual
sense of Scripture expounded in the manifest places of Scripture
and agreeable to the Apostles' Creed, the Ten Commandments,
and the general sentences and axioms of every main point in
divinity."

[9] *Institutes,* as cited, I.12.

[10] Barr, *Fundamentalism*, London: SCM Press, 1977, pp. 1, 37,
40, 51 ff., etc.

[11] Stephen Davis, *The Debate About the Bible*, Philadelphia: West-
mintster Press, 1977, p. 116. Harold Lindsell justifiably observes
that this passage "opens a door so wide that everything can pass
through. The Trinity, the deity of Christ, the virgin birth and
the bodily resurrection of Jesus from the dead can easily be
dispensed with. Right now there are a number of scholars who
have what seems to them to be perfectly valid reasons to say
Jesus is not God" (*The Bible in the Balance*, Grand Rapids: Zondervan, 1979, p. 54).

[12] Ed. James Montgomery Boice, *The Foundation of Biblical Authority*, Grand Rapids: Zondervan, 1978, p. 54, note 10.

[13] *The Inspiration of Scripture*, Philadelphia: Westminster Press;
Scripture, Tradition and Infallibility, Grand Rapids: Eerdmans.

[14] *Constitution on Revelation*, chapter 3, section 11: *The Documents of Vatican II*, ed. Walter M. Abbott, London: Geoffrey
Chapman, 1966, p. 119; ed. Austin P. Flannery, Grand Rapids:
Eerdmans, 1975, p. 757. "The statement, like so many others at
the Council, is a compromise. It is deliberately ambiguous so

that the old and the new views of the Bible can alike appeal to it. But Rome had not been ambiguous on this point before; therefore, it should be considered as a victory for the progressives" (Clark Pinnock in *God's Inerrant Word*, p. 147; cf. J.W. Montgomery, *op. cit.*, pp. 263 ff., and J. I. Packer, *The Foundation of Biblical Authority*, pp. 74 ff.).

[15]See Pinnock, "Limited Inerrancy," in *God's Inerrant Word*, pp. 143 ff., esp. pp. 145-150. Harold Lindsell says that the statement of the Lausanne Covenant that Scripture is "inerrant in all that it affirms" has been subscribed by some in "limited inerrancy" terms: *op. cit.*, pp. 52, 85. Certainly, this would be possible.

[16]See note 1 for bibliographical details.

[17]Grand Rapids: Zondervan, 1976, 1979.

[18]Waco: Word Books, 1977. The volume *Scripture, Tradition, and Interpretation: Essays Presented to Everett F. Harrison*, ed. W. W. Gasque and W. S. LaSor, Grand Rapids: Eerdmans, 1978, should also be consulted for evidence on Fuller Seminary thinking about the Bible.

[19]See note 12 for bibliographical details.

[20]The Statement is printed in full in *Journal of the Evangelical Theological Society*, December 1978 (XXI.4), pp. 289 ff., and in J. I. Packer, *God Has Spoken*, London: Hodder & Stoughton, and Downers Grove, Ill.; InterVarsity Press, pp. 139 ff. Half of it is reproduced in Lindsell, *op. cit.*, pp. 366 ff.

[21]Grand Rapids: Eerdmans, 1975; cf. pp. 181 ff., 265. Jack B. Rogers expounds Berkouwer's teaching with clarity and enthusiasm in *Scripture, Tradition and Interpretation*, pp. 70 ff.

[22]See note 20 for bibliographical details.

[23]Some of what follows is based on *God Has Spoken*, pp. 110 ff.

[24]This proposal is about a century old. Thus, for example, T. H. Walker, in his *Life of James Denney*, tells how in debate in the Glasgow United Free Presbytery in 1904 Denney, having been criticized for rejecting the Davidic authorship of Psalm 110, said he could profess faith in the infallibility of Scripture—meaning, its power to bring us to God and to eternal life—but not in its "literal accuracy and inerrancy" (p. 91; cf. Denney's statement in the General Assembly, 1891: "The word of God infallibly carries God's power to save men's souls. That is the only kind of infallibility I believe in"; quoted from ed. James Moffatt, *Letters of Principal James Denney to his Family and Friends*, London: Hodder and Stoughton, [1922], p. 23). Other late nineteenth-century Presbyterians such as W. Robertson Smith, C. A. Briggs, A. B. Bruce, T. M. Lindsay and Marcus Dods would speak the same way: Cf. H. D. McDonald, *Theories of Revelation: an Historical Study, 1860-1960*, London: George Allen & Unwin, 1963, chapter 6, pp. 196-217; Jack Rogers and Donald K. McKim, *The Au-*

thority and Interpretation of the Bible, San Francisco: Harper & Row, 1979, pp. 380 ff.

[25]*Inst.* I.vii.5.

[26]*op. cit.*, pp. 181 ff.

[27]Unless the translator, who tells us that he abridged the work by a third from its two-volume Dutch original by deleting Berkouwer's "interaction with persons holding other viewpoints," cut out the relevant references. I am not able to check this.

[28]pp. 182 f.

[29]p. 265.

[30]If Lindsell is right in alleging (on a hearsay basis, apparently) that Berkouwer doubts the historicity of Adam and Eve and the reality of hell, then I should have differences with him also about the meaning of a number of biblical texts. See Lindsell, *op. cit.*, pp. 33, 78, 222, 341.

[31]Cited from the Exposition. Compare the Articles of Affirmation and Denial, xiii: "We affirm the propriety of using inerrancy as a theological term with reference to the complete truthfulness of Scripture. We deny . . . that inerrancy is negated by Biblical phenomena such as a lack of modern technical precision, irregularities of grammar or spelling, observational descriptions of nature, the reporting of falsehoods (e.g., the lies of Satan), the use of hyperbole and round numbers, the topical arrangement of material, variant selections of material in parallel accounts, or the use of free citations." And Article xviii: "We affirm that the text of Scripture is to be interpreted by grammatico-historical exegesis, taking account of its literary forms and devices, and that Scripture is to interpret Scripture."

[32]*Asynchutōs, atreptōs, adiairetōs, achōristōs.*

[33]"Must the Bible Be an Infallible Book?" pp. 7-9.

Chapter 4

[1]*"Fundamentalism" and the Word of God*, London: Inter-Varsity Press and Grand Rapids: Eerdmans, 1958, pp. 152 ff. See also James Barr, *The Bible in the Modern World*, London: SCM Press, 1973, pp. 1-12, and Brevard S. Childs, *Biblical Theology in Crisis*, Philadelphia: Westminster Press, 1970, pp. 13-87, 103 f. Childs' footnotes are in effect a superb bibliography of the "biblical theology" movement from North American perspective. Cf. J. D. Smart, *The Past, Present and Future of Biblical Theology*, Philadelphia: Westminster Press, 1979.

[2]*op. cit.*, p. 158.

[3]cf. Childs, *op. cit.*, pp. 51-87. Barr, *op. cit.*, *The Bible in the Modern World*, p. 10, classifies the questions which "biblical

theology" is nowadays felt to have left unanswered as follows:

    (i) Questions about *relevance* ... how ... can material from that very different biblical situation be decisive for our problems?

    (ii) Questions about *communicability* ... how ... can we expect that which was meaningful to (the men of the Bible) to communicate the same meaning to us?

    (iii) Questions about *limitations:* The Bible is a limited set of books, chosen partly by accident and coming from a limited segment of the total history of the church; how can its insights be decisive for us in any way which is qualitatively different from that which attaches to other books and other times?

    (iv) Questions about *isolation:* How can the Bible be assigned a position qualitatively different from all the other factors which come into the mind ... when decisions about faith and ethics have to be taken?

    (v) Questions about *our responsibility:* The task of the church is to say what the church and Christians believe today. This responsibility is evaded or distorted if we suppose that our main responsibility is to restate, to reinterpret, or to make our thoughts dependent upon, what was believed by the men of biblical times.

This summary is as precise as it is provocative.

[4]The "canonical" approach of Brevard S. Childs, as seen in his *Commentary on Exodus,* Old Testament Library, Philadelphia: Westminster Press, 1974, and his *Introduction to the Old Testament as Scripture,* Philadelphia: Fortress Press, 1979, seems to me a very important step in the right direction, though Childs might not agree with my statement in the text.

[5]Above, chapter 1.

[6]See J. R. Gieselmann, "Scripture, Tradition and the Church: an Ecumenical Problem" in *Christianity Divided*, ed. D. J. Callahan, H. A. Obermann, D. J. O'Hanlon, London: Sheed & Ward, 1962, pp. 39 ff. Trent said that gospel doctrine is given us in written books and *(et)* unwritten traditions. The Council agreed on the non-committal "et" as an alternative to a proposal to say that doctrine comes to us partly in the Scriptures and partly in unwritten traditions *(partim ... partim ...);* thus it was left open to regard the traditions as expository of rather than supplementary to what is written.

[7]Abbott, *op. cit.* chapter 2, pp. 114-118; Flannery, pp. 753-56.

[8]In his article, "Biblical Theology" in *Lexicon für Theologie und Kirche,* ed. J. Hofer and K. Rahner, Freiburg: Vertag Herder, vol 2, 1958, pp. 449 f., Rahner affirms that the proclamation of the church's faith must be founded on Scripture, as the basis and authority for faith and life, and that Scripture stands above tradition as the only *norma non normanda* [standard not subject to another standard], and that nothing should be held and taught in the church that is not motivated and sanctioned by Scripture.

[9]See the report, "Tradition and Traditions," in *Faith and*

Order Findings, ed. Paul S. Minear, London: SCM Press, 1963; also, Max Thurian, *Visible Unity and Tradition,* London: Darton, Longman & Todd, 1964, with the bibliographical notes on p. 53.

[10]"Recommendations for Diocesan Ecumenical Commissions," circulated by the Roman Catholic Ecumenical Commission for England and Wales and dated May, 1968, called for the forming of house groups of Roman Catholics and others who would "start by discussing what various Christian traditions have in common" and go on "to pray together, and to join in Bible-study." Roman Catholics were to "take the initiative in starting such groups, in the conviction that they have much to give, though also something to learn" (p. 16).

[11]G. B. Bentley, *The Resurrection of the Bible,* London: Dacre Press, 1940, p. 1.

[12]New York: Doubleday and Harmondsworth: Penguin, 1957. See also G. Hebert, *The Bible from Within,* London: Oxford University Press, 1950; "The Holy Bible: Its Authority and Message" in *The Lambeth Conference, 1958,* London: SPCK, 1958, 2.1 ff.; H. H. Rowley, *The Rediscovery of the Old Testament,* London: James Clarke and Philadelphia: Westminster Press, 1945; G. E. Wright, *The Challenge of Israel's Faith,* Chicago: University of Chicago Press, 1944; Paul S. Minear, *Eyes of Faith: a Study in the Biblical Point of View,* Philadelphia: Westminster Press, 1946; W. Neil, *The Rediscovery of the Bible,* London: Hodder & Stoughton, 1954; etc.

[13]See B. B. Warfield, "God-inspired Scripture," *op. cit.,* pp. 245-96—an article dating from 1900, but still definitive.

[14]See C. H. Dodd, *According to the Scriptures,* London: Nisbet, 1952; R. V. G. Tasker, *The Old Testament in the New Testament,* 2nd ed., London: SCM Press, 1954; E. Earle Ellis, *Paul's Use of the Old Testament,* Edinburgh: Oliver & Boyd, 1957; B. Lindars, *New Testament Apologetic,* London: SCM Press, 1961; F. F. Bruce, *This is That,* Exeter: Paternoster Press, 1968; etc.

[15]Article, "Inspiration" in *The New Bible Dictionary,* ed. J. D. Douglas *et al.,* London: Inter-Varsity Fellowship, 1962, p. 564.

[16]*pulchra omnium partium inter se consensio (Institutio* I.viii.1).

[17]See R. E. Davies, *The Problem of Authority in the Continental Reformers,* London: Epworth Press, 1946, pp. 114 ff.; E. A. Dowey, *The Knowledge of God in Calvin's Theology,* New York: Columbia University Press, 1952, pp. 101 ff.; John Murray, *Calvin on Scripture and Divine Sovereignty,* Philadelphia: Presbyterian and Reformed Publishing Co., chapters 1 and 2; J. I. Packer in *John Calvin,* ed. G. E. Duffield, Abingdon: Sutton Courtenay Press, 1966, pp. 162 ff. and *op. cit.,* J. W. Montgomery, pp. 95 ff.; H. J. Forstman, *Word and Spirit,* Stanford: Stanford University Press, 1962, pp. 49 ff.

[18]Abbot, *op. cit.*, chapter 3, sections 11, 13, pp. 118-21; Flannery, pp. 756-58.

[19]Cf. chapter II, note 14, p. 153 above.

[20]J. A. T. Robinson's important book, *Redating the New Testament*, London: SCM Press, 1976, shows that it is not necessary to posit a date later than A.D. 70 for any New Testament book.

[21]For a survey of the very little information about Jesus that can be gleaned extra-biblically, see Roderic Dunkerley, *Beyond the Gospels*, Harmondsworth: Penguin, 1957.

[22]Callahan *et al.*, *op. cit.*, pp. 21 f. Cullmann's article dates from 1953.

[23]H. N. Ridderbos, *The Authority of the New Testament Scriptures*, Philadelphia: Presbyterian and Reformed Publishing Co., 1963, pp. 14, 44; cf. Berkouwer, *op. cit.*, pp. 83 ff.

[24]On the history of the formation of the New Testament canon, see J. N. Birdsall, "Canon of the New Testament," in *New Bible Dictionary*, pp. 194 ff.; H. N. Ridderbos, "The Canon of the New Testament," in *Revelation and the Bible*, ed. C. F. H. Henry, Grand Rapids: Baker Book House, 1958, pp. 187 ff.

[25]*Conversations between the Church of England and the Methodist Church*, London: SPCK and Epworth Press, 1963, p. 58 (from the Dissentient View).

[26]Rupert E. Davies, *Religious Authority in an Age of Doubt*, London: Epworth Press, 1968, p. 214.

[27]In 1951 the volume *Biblical Authority for Today*, ed. A. Richardson and W. Schweizer, Philadelphia: Westminster Press and London: SCM Press, which the Commission on Faith and Order of the World Council of Churches had sponsored, offered a consensus by fifteen leading biblical scholars on guiding principles for biblical interpretation (pp. 240-44). In 1967 Erich Dinkler concluded his report to the Commission on Faith and Order as follows: "When the World Council of Churches was founded, there was a strong hope . . . that . . . the Bible would be read more and more along the same lines, provided by the development of the so-called 'biblical theology. . . .' Now, two decades later, attention is increasingly drawn to the diversity amongst or even contradiction between biblical writers. . . . As a consequence the hope that the churches would find themselves to have . . . a common understanding of the one biblical message has been fading, even to such an extent that in the eyes of some the new exegetical developments seem to undermine the raison d'être of the ecumenical movement" (quoted from Childs, *Biblical Theology in Crisis*, pp. 81 f.).

[28]See the books listed in note 12 above, and from the Roman Catholic side L. Bouyer, *The Meaning of Sacred Scripture*, London: Darton, Longman & Todd, 1960, and Notre Dame: University of

Notre Dame Press, 1958; C. Charlier, *The Christian Approach to the Bible*, London: Sands, 1958.

[29]Augustine, *Confessions* viii.29.

[30]Luther, *Works*, Weimar: Böhlau, 54.179 ff.

[31]*Journal of John Wesley*, 24 May 1738.

[32]*Romans* (Tyndale Commentary), London: Tyndale Press, 1963, p. 60.

[33]*Church Dogmatics I.i: The Doctrine of the Word of God*, tr. G. T. Thomson, Edinburgh: T. & T. Clark, 1936, p. 120; criticized by, e.g., H. Cunliffe-Jones, *The Authority of the Biblical Revelation*, London: James Clarke, 1945, chapter 8.

[34]Childs, *Biblical Theology in Crisis*, p. 103.

[35]Cf. the Chicago Statement on Biblical Inerrancy: above, II, pp. 48 ff., and note 20, p.154.